Flotsam and Jetsam

FLOTSAM AND JETSAM
Wit and Wisdom of Betsy Cochran

Eelman's Press
Ithaca, NY

Design by Larry Clarkberg.

Photos on pages, 60, 69, 77, 79, 100 (cave) and 130 by Teresita Cochran.
Photo on page 70 by Michael Poniatowski.
Cover illustration (repeated on page 84) and illustration on page 152 by
Helen Lyman. Other illustrations in Section 4 by Nanvan Hansen.

ISBN 0-9747053-0-6

Published by Eelman's Press
205 Haller Blvd.
Ithaca, NY 14850

First printing 2003.

Dedication:

Off Sailing

I am glad I found your poem
on the desk, among papers
partly tended-to.
"The quiet—
broken only by
the intoxicating susurrus
of waves under the bow,
and the white wake streaming out behind."
It tells me where you are.

Contents

Foreword

If you have found these words, then you are on the threshold of a wonderful, refreshing experience; spending time with Betsy Cochran.

She was not at the epicenter of world-shaking events of the past half-century—as defined by macro-historians, anyway. Her literary ambitions were not grandiose, her style not austere or sharply chiseled in the way of the moderns.

She was, as Gertrude Stein might say, where she was. That place is gentle, personal, whimsical, keenly observed, humorously rendered, constantly engaged, drawing strength both from her home Cape Cod and the looping orbits of her family solar system.

Over and over, her stories delight, surprise, and then linger long after the page is turned, bringing an unexpected smile a day later, a week later. It's as if her subjects and observations are wonderful bits and pieces of this life washed into our world from hers, left behind on a high tide of her own making.

Once she points us toward her subjects, it seems so clear that of course, there they are, wonderful stuff right at our feet. And yet we didn't notice them until she guided us to the shore, took us along with her on a Betsy Cochran version of a beachcombing expedition.

So this collection is aptly named.

Beach metaphors are only one way these stories link to Betsy's adopted home, Cape Cod. Betsy is perhaps the highest example of what people on the sandspit call a "washashore," meaning someone who was born elsewhere, but found her way to the Cape and came to call it home. For Betsy it was marriage and family that brought her here, but then she came to embrace the place because it offered her so much, and she wanted to give back. These stories are one way she did, to the delight of readers spanning 50 years.

To find them gathered together within one jacket is like finding a beautiful quilt carefully stitched from fabrics culled over decades, arranged so that each small square links nicely to the next, but each also is allowed to display its colors. And also like a quilt, these stories will warm you up.

Call it coincidence, luck, or fate, but Betsy's style and personality suited her to the Cape she has come to know so well. This is not a place that draws all kinds of attention to itself, that bowls people over at the first glance. This is a subtle little finger at the fringe of a big continent, its beauty often emerging only after many associations, its landscape low and repetitive, its depth and humor not obvious or trumpeted. Yet it rewards anyone willing to slow down, observe, and participate. That's what Betsy has done, and that's what she offers, too.

No doubt she'll be embarrassed by words like these, p'shaw them as making too much of what she probably considers to be a nice but rather small collection of musings. I can hear her now, saying something self-effacing, wondering whether they really stand up to time's passing, whether anyone other than the people who already love her will find much in the stories.

She shouldn't fret about any of that, and she shouldn't be embarrassed by the celebration this book represents. Betsy Cochran is a writer full of joy and humor, invention and insight. Reading this collection is like sitting on a wraparound porch overlooking a bay tossed by a late summer breeze, in the company of a great friend who manages to point out something fresh, and celebrate something almost taken for granted.

Thank you, Betsy, for doing that for so many of us, over and over again.

—*Seth Rolbein*
Fall, 2003

(Seth Rolbein is editor and publisher of The Cape Cod Voice, and former editor of The Cape Codder.)

Acknowledgements

This book embodies a collection of columns, light verse and occasional articles, most of which appeared in The Cape Codder newspaper between 1950 and 2000, while Malcolm Hobbs was Editor in Chief. The column headings were *Ironic Board*, *Backwash*, and *Focus*.

My ghost-writer, Norma, a soft-shell clam whose haunts include the flats that fringe Pleasant Bay Narrows, appears here on the cover (at her insistence). See Section Four for various dialogues with her.

The pieces included are not in the order in which they were written, but instead are grouped loosely according to general topics addressed.

Thanks is given to The Cape Codder newspaper, whose archives were made accessible for the gathering of many of these writings, and which has graciously permitted the publication of them.

My sister, Helen C. Lyman brought Norma the Clam visibility by providing her portrait, for which both Norma and I are grateful, and my niece Nanvan Hansen captured more active unposed shots of her.

Larry Clarkberg did a wonderful job of designing the writings, photos, and illustrations into an attractive book, for which I am most grateful.

Finally, appreciation goes to my family of five progeny, who provided much of the grist for my mill and the research and publishing assistance that led to this book.

—*Betsy Cochran*
Summer, 2003

Preface

If I ever hear my name
echo down the Hall of Fame,
or if I shall ever be on
voted lists for Obli-vion;

If I make a lot of money
let it be for being funny.

Let my rivals think it hard
keeping up with such a card.
Let me roll in wealth and riches,
keeping fellowman in stitches.

'Til I earn an epitaph,
with the words 'here lies a laugh.'

—Betsy Cochran, 1938

Making a Career of It

Making a Career of It

Motherhood as a Career

I tried to kiss my elbow when I was six years old because someone said that it would turn me into a boy, and I had just found out that when it came to picking career choices I was on the wrong team. (Motherhood was a choice, but was it a career?)

I knew boys my age were destined to be doctor, lawyer, merchant chief or President when they grew up. These were not unrealistic goals for them. After all, JFK was a boy my age, though I didn't know it at the time. Boys had a panoply of choices and destinies.

But what could I be, as a girl? None of the above, in those days between WWI and WWII. Women could find subservient work as stenographers or in libraries, elementary schools or hospitals, often part time, not likely to stimulate those yearning for a career outside the home, but helpful to those needing to be self-supporting often because they weren't married.

Society's rules were: men go off to work all day to support themselves, their wives and children; women marry. Marrying for love was romantic expectation, highly touted in the popular new movies. Marrying for support came into the picture too, necessarily part of the agenda whether hidden or spoken. And marrying was the only acceptable precursor to having babies. Making a go of marriage and motherhood was a woman's career. This was an expected goal to be rewarded by richness of life, rather than a salary. A wife might get a household allowance, but rarely a bank account under her control alone.

Well, I wasn't about to accept such rules unchallenged, but I never did get to kiss my elbow. It was so near, and yet so far. I went to college as a possible route to an interesting career, majored in History and Literature of England, and came out with the conviction that war was not the solution to world problems—just as the Battle of Britain was storming the radio newscasts.

Britain needed our support, whether we were doves or hawks. I took a menial job at the British Consulate in Boston clipping New England press stories that showed local attitudes toward the war in Europe, and taking dictation and typing reports of these attitudes, to be sent to England and New York City.

This wasn't my dream career, especially when my boss (the British wife of a Harvard archaeologist) had me commuting to her home rather than the office, because of her motherly duties, and would sometimes give me household chores to do like walking the dog. Before my first year was out she had added twin baby girls to her family, and I was thinking of getting married myself.

Pearl Harbor was attacked less than three months after my marriage, and our twins arrived seven months after that. I remember looking at them lying on my hospital bed. Together they weighed fifteen magnificent pounds. I was proud of that, and there they were, red, squirming, hiccupping and helpless, and I thought, "Now, what?"

I was the baby in my family, and here I was totally inexperienced with infants. Baby kittens were the closest I'd come. It amounted to a crash course in babies for me, as my husband and I wound up with five of them in five and a half years. Luckily he knew about them, having had five younger brothers and sisters. At least five kids per family was de rigueur among his siblings. We didn't worry about overpopulation in those days. That kind of thing might happen in Asia, but here there was even talk of the baby boom replacing the losses overseas.

People would ask us how we managed, at times, though the answer was obvious: the house was always a mess. The kids were very convenient cover for our housekeeping inadequacies. You do what you have to do because it's there. Luck played a very big part in our case. We lived on Cape Cod near Pleasant Bay, which is a live laboratory for kids to explore, relatively safe, but challenging. We had no serious health problems. I didn't have to work outside. The children were close enough in age to like doing the same sorts of things together most of the time.

We lived off-season in a summer house, heated only by a space heater and fireplace, for our first twelve years on the Cape, but had to leave it in the summer. Four summers we traveled out to Boulder, Colorado, in a Jeep station wagon with a small swivel-wheeled farm trailer full of camping gear out behind. My husband got his Masters in Guidance at the University there, and on weekends the whole family climbed mountains with the college Mountain Recreation Group, earning an honorary Doctor of Mountaineering degree collectively thereby, presented at a cap and gown ceremony (paper plate mortarboards and poncho gowns). This was peak experience.

There were hills and valleys over the years, of course. The children got more collective than personal attention. When they began to leave home for schools, colleges or jobs they remained nostalgic about the Cape, but haven't chosen to live here. Yet.

So what happened to the big career? It turned out to be avocation after all: part time work for The Cape Codder; teaching and counseling at Sea Pines School and later for Salzburg International Preparatory School and Sea Pines Abroad, after the flock had flown. No supermom, no big career, and no regret. We have outstanding, not infrequent reunions, and viewed as a fulfilling vocation, I would much rather be a mother and grandmother, as it happened to me, than be President.

The Cape, and the world outside, changed rapidly through those years, as did society. After the war, women were more widely accepted at work. Technology simplified housekeeping. Population soared. Our granddaughters see marriage as an option rather than a necessity.

To be a mother at home nowadays is a privilege most can't afford, nor can they afford expensive day care. This is a dilemma society has yet to solve.

Please Take Your Seats

I can't remember my ancient history teacher, but I remember where I sat, third row back on the aisle, beside Pat. I remember where lots of the others sat too...Jill and Olivia in the next to last row center (the most strategic spot for passing notes)...Alice, left aisle, halfway down, where she could soften wads of modeling clay on the radiator. Kitty, of course, sat right in front, peering at the teacher through her thick glasses. She would! We didn't altogether despise her, though—we pitied her too. She couldn't really help the way she was, and someone once told me that, when the others weren't around, she wasn't nearly so hard to take...even had a rudimentary sense of humor. I'm afraid we never took the trouble to find out. It never even occurred to us that she may have been sitting in the front row because she was so nearsighted, but that could have been one of the reasons anyhow.

We all knew where she fitted in, and she seemed quite self-satisfied (which gave her a fan-club of one, at least). Any of us could have drawn one of these diagrams sociologists make showing where everyone stands in relation to his peers, and there would have been a distinct correlation between the diagram and where we sat (with the saddest cases near the front). I didn't particularly like my seat—it was too near the blackboard—but Pat had saved it for me on opening day (I was always late) and from then on the matter was settled.

The same sort of thing went on in algebra class. There Pat and I were in the fourth row, just off center, since our ratings among the kids in our Algebra section were different from our standing in the Ancient History group. Here there was a less demanding environment, and we emerged as leaders of the opposition, or so we felt. We liked being considered way out. I'll never forget the day we came in wearing that brownish purple nail polish. On me it looked ludicrous, but somehow it made her look more like a panther than ever. Louise was the only one in the front row in that class—Louise with her pale eyes and skin, her stiff black hair waved in ridges, and her strange plaintive voice that made your spine shiver. She reminded me of a polynomial fall of Xs, (only she used to pronounce it polynomee-el). I said so in a note to Pat, who nodded and drew an appropriate illustration that broke me up completely. We certainly could be insufferable when we put our minds to it.

This was the way it was in all our classes where seats hadn't been assigned to us. We kind of fell into seats that fit our group relationship, and kept the same arrangements going all year. It was comfortable to know where you sat, and it saved you the anxiety of daily decisions. Besides, if you took someone else's seat they'd let you know about it fast. "That's my seat," they'd say, looking hostile, "I'm sitting there."

I used to think of the school as regimented, but actually we did a lot of the regimenting ourselves in this way. We kept reinforcing behavior patterns that probably started in kindergarten and were to last a lifetime. When we were through school it was natural to establish seating pattern habits at club and association meetings. Everyone knows perfectly well where they will sit at Town Meeting, for instance, and knows where to look for the others as well. It's the same way at church—in fact some churches encourage this sort of thing. So, too, at PTA, and so on.

I recently signed up for a course in Learning Theory, and on the first day after milling around for a few minutes before the hour we each gravitated to an appropriately situated chair which was to be the one we would claim for the rest of the course. Oh, I admit there have been a few substitutions and one or two of us is occasionally caught off-side, but by and large our lineup has remained constant—a sort of reversed T formation.

Memories of Ancient History class flood back to me as we take our seats. The pattern is similar, though the faces have changed. A couple of undergraduates are sitting in the third row back on the aisle. Two ex-marines are in the next-to-last row, center. And I find myself right up front, peering at the professor through my thick glasses, though I'm not in the least near-sighted...

Faith

I first got religion
when I found the kitten
after two days of searching—
the one that mattered most
of a litter of five.

Five. That's about what I was then.
I tested God, and He measured up.

It could happen any time, but not always.
Just often enough.
Random reinforcement.

These days I sometimes think all there is
is hunting for things.

Sometimes it's just letting miracles happen.

Spring Cleaning Or Spring Fever?

Women there are, born with a good housecleaning stamp of approval on their foreheads, who would much rather cavort around with a vacuum cleaner or shampoo a rug than watch a tulip unfold. They act this way throughout the year, and when spring comes they just secrete more adrenaline to jet fuel the engine and rocket around the house terrifying man and beast. They know what to do at this time of year, so my advice is not for them.

Then there are the rest of us whose eyes mist over at the sight of the first dandelion, who yearn secretly for a skip rope or a game of hopscotch as soon as peepers start peeping, and who shed the house along with winter underwear, as a cat sheds hairs, come spring.

The last time the downstairs rug was shampooed at our house we took a movie of it: it was that much of an event. It was after we had gone out and stayed longer than we expected, and came back to find that the puppies had—well, you know. So we all got together and hauled the rug out to the blacktopped parking area where we could play a hose on it and have the water (and everything it took with it) drain out into the bushes. We sprinkled it liberally with detergent to make nice bubbles, and the kids put on bathing suits so they could have water fights while leaping around on the rug to dislodge deep-down dirt. They were teenagers then, and really knew how to leap about. While one worked the hose the others each did his own brand of acrobatics and interpretive dancing. We got cartwheels, back flips and handstands, pirouettes, jetes and entrechats—the whole works. It began to rain in the middle of it all which added to the hilarity, much of which we recorded on deathless celluloid. When we run that old movie now we have hysterics all over again, especially running it backwards during all the somersaults and back flips.

The sun came out again after a day or two and dried the rug, so we hauled it back in. No doubt about it, it was lighter in hue than it had been, and had lost some of the seedy mottled buffalo look it used to have. We had done a good thorough job. It was an impressive change, but the rug had shrunk about three inches all around, and the holes that had been cut in it for the heating vents no longer landed on the vents, so we had to cut more.

That was a once-in-a-lifetime performance, and we never did shampoo that rug again. After a few years we had it replaced with wall-to-wall carpeting in a good shade that doesn't show dirt, and we plant a chair over any spot that does appear, which gives a free-form quality to the furniture arrangement.

I mention all this to show that I do know what I'm talking about when it comes to rug cleaning and the like. Some people have a way of talking about spring cleaning as if it were as inevitable as the income tax deadline. Nowhere near, not around here. If you want to avoid it at apple blossom time, sharpen up your rationalizing. "Why spring cleaning?" you may ask. "Wouldn't fall cleaning be more to the point, getting the house ready to live in all winter?" Then fling open the windows for a change of air and take off for a day at the herring run, or a dig at the garden. After all, if you did spring clean the house, it would get all dirty again with spring mud and summer sand.

If you want to get credit for spring cleaning, and cop out at the same time, you can try getting someone else to do it, but that's expensive. Cleaning persons come high these days and require your equipment to be in good repair, on the ready. If you think you can get your kids to do it, good luck. They'll cost a lot too, and be lazy about moving the furniture. Kids take economics in high schools these days.

Another approach, when it comes to moving furniture, is to buy enough at yard sales in the fall to carry through the winter, and sell it at yardsales in the spring. During the summer you camp out. This gives variety to the scene, and makes yardsale-browsing meaningful. If you can spend your time playing the money market instead of spring housecleaning, you may be able to buy everything new from our advertisers, whenever you want to freshen things up.

It's curious that the quality of pain conjured up by the word "fever" as compared with "cleaning" reverses itself when you attach "spring" to each of them.

Personally, I'll take my "cleaning" plain, unadorned, and only occasionally, but I want my fever lying in a bed of hyacinth, fanned by April breezes.

Welcome

On gala occasions when we entertain
with the front porch alight, calling guests from the rain,
with deadly precision, they aim their attack
through the trash ridden shed, and the door at the back.
They emerge brave but shaken, intrepid but paler
through having encountered the depth of our squalor.

And yet to the front door instead of the rear,
the children bring children, and all of their gear,
and everything living from quahogs to snakes,
and all sorts of hardware, like guns, rods, and rakes,
and mice barely conscious, and ducks hardly dead.
No wonder the livingroom looks like the shed!

No wonder that Santa Claus, ever astute,
chooses a far more conservative route!

—

First Things First

It was never, "My, how nice your house looks!" when people stopped by to see us and wanted to say something kind. It was, "My dear, how do you do it with so many kids and animals, and a job, too?"—a rhetorical question asked as they picked their way among scattered footgear, piles of dirty laundry and pans of half-eaten dog food. (That was before children and animals dispersed.)

"Well, ah—" I would mutter, blushing. With the evidence at hand, to say more was redundant. But redundant or not, one day, instead of paying bills and making out shopping lists, I was possessed to describe it on paper in black (plenty of black) and white, as follows:

"Never mind the job part," I began. For the rest, it's just a matter of organization. Just get things lined up, and there they are, lined up. All you have to remember is, first things first.

So Friday comes, the day I set aside for housework, and after the traumatic experience of getting the family off, I slump over my coffee and whip up a schedule for myself. First things first, I remind myself briskly and often.

All right, what's the first thing? Well, obviously the dishes come first. There they sit, food hardening on the plates. But now it occurs to me that while I sit writing I could have the washer and dryer going, fluffing up clothes for the weary week ahead, and I could have a nutritious stew simmering on the back of the stove, and dessert bubbling in the oven.

Apparently, then, the schedule should not be the first thing. I make off for the laundry taking my coffee along to restore confidence. I find the washer full of wet clothes and the dryer full of dry ones. All the clothes baskets are full of clothes waiting to be sorted, and the top of the dryer is the only place the boys could find to build their models, so I heap the clean clothes out on the floor, which, incidentally, needs vacuuming.

Out with the old, in with the new. I finally start the machines, pick the clothes off the floor and perch them precariously on one of the full baskets, braced against the wall. Then up to the kitchen to begin scraping carrots for the stew. The prickly sensation of half-a-dozen runs sprung simultaneously in my stockings reminds me that the kitten hasn't been fed. I remove her like a burr from my shin, holding her, carrot and scraper in my right hand while mixing her milk and kitty chow with my left. Unhappily I am right-handed. As I mop up I note distractedly that the kitten should have come before everything.

Back to carrot-scraping, with the peelings forming a shaggy blanket over the breakfast dishes. Shouldn't I have started out by cleaning up after breakfast? Well, wasn't that first on the schedule? You see, I really do need that schedule, and there's no point putting it off when it's needed right away. That's the thing about carrot-scraping. It gives you a chance to think.

Just then the telephone rings. Ten or fifteen minutes later I hang up, run down to the laundry and put the wet clothes in the dryer, which has to be emptied first. Finding my coffee cup there on the window sill, I take it up with me, back to the sink. But where is the carrot scraper? After a frantic search I decide it would be easier to find if I did the dishes. Doing them, I consider what a difference it makes to my morale and efficiency to have things tidied up and squared away.

So knowing that the most distracting mess in my house is the confusion of newspapers and magazines that flow over the living room coffee table onto the floor, I now approach it, warily, having been through this before. Can anyone sort newspapers and magazines without stopping to read here and there?

And so it goes, with time out for lunch, until the children come home from school. By then the stew may be underway except for the carrots, and most of the dishes are done, though a couple needed soaking. The telephone rings again. My husband says he is bringing a couple home for refreshments around five. Ah-there's the carrot scraper! On the telephone book.

By 4 pm, after the children have spread their peanut butter, jelly and chocolate milk over the kitchen, I go into high gear. After all, something has to be done before these people arrive. I wind up and start spurting around, letting out intermittent bleats and moans.

"What's the matter, mother?" a daughter asks with polite concern. I tell her about the guests and add, "What's more, they're perfectly likely to want to see the house, and a look at your room will give them an idea of the hog wallow we live in."

So she goes to her room, collects her wash, and tosses it out into the hall, just as the boys come in caked with mud, leading the dog. "Let her stay in for a while," they say.

At five o'clock, as our guests pick their way among the piles of dirty clothes, footgear, and pans of half-eaten dog food, the wife says to me, kindly, "I don't see how you do it, with all you have to do!"

First things first, I mutter to myself. Out loud, "we like to have the house look lived-in," I say.

It's a lie, of course, or was then. Now, I'm not so sure.

Farm Labor Day

There's nothing to running the house when the family is away. It's so peaceful. You can keep your mind on what you're doing and forget what you're not doing. Goodness, I could handle it with my hands tied behind my back if I were a little better at knots, but I can't even tie my hands in front.

So I was really living it up this weekend, with all the kids and my husband up to no good somewhere else. My sister and brother-in-law were here for supper and we ate what I liked for a change. It happened to be curried chicken, which the children hate, and chutney, which they call gutney, but they weren't around to complain. Then we went to the theatre and came back full of carefree chatter and were about to retire when we remembered the animals. They hadn't been fed. Not usually my job, you understand, but with everyone away...

Well, my sister is very game and fond of animals, thank heavens. "Let's go," she said. And heck, there's nothing to feeding the animals. I could do it with my hands tied behind my back, provided there were a couple of animal lovers like my sister with me for company. So we set out, after kicking off our pumps and putting on sneakers, but I'm getting ahead of my story. Before we left the house, the guinea pigs, who live beside the ping pong table on the lower level of our split level, in a split level of their own, tuned up with their "Queep, queep, queep." I sauntered into the kitchen to think things over and lay out a plan. Two cats and three kittens came in with me, rubbing and occasionally clawing my ankles. The message came through to me. The situation called for spontaneous organizational leadership, so I fumbled around the refrigerator for milk while shouting to my sister (who hears just as well when I speak softly) that I would feed the cats while she did the guinea pigs (since she was already starting down to them with a bowl of tossed salad). She had fed the dogs while I was grappling with my sneakers.

All was going well I felt. It's great to know that you can be left in charge. Some time later we set out to do the horses and goats. I had a latent blast of foresight and went back for a flashlight. Then came the question of whose car to take, hers or mine. We settled for hers without wrangling because although it had a lot of hardware on the back seat, including a saw which had to be maneuvered around, it was parked in a place that was easier to get out of without running over kittens. The dog Pooh, having finished his Pard, jumped into the back seat on top of the saw, ready for the fray.

We drove the few yards to the horse corral and crawled under the barbed wire like old G.I.'s. I held the flashlight with one hand and gestured with the other telling her what to do. Efficiency in an operation of this kind depends on the right orders at the right time.

"You open the door and go into the barn," I said briskly " while I shine the flashlight. The horses, Sybil and Princess, helped us along the manured path with affectionate nudging. Neither I nor my sister had ever been on what you might call nudging terms with horses, but we held our own. Pooh barked hysterically.

My sister opened the door and started to go in, and the horses and Pooh started in too. So I shut the door to keep them out, but that left her in the dark. So I opened the door a crack and handed her the flashlight but then how could she fill both pails and hold the flashlight at the same time and bring them out along with a pail for the goats? So I joined her in there, closing the door behind me. It wasn't exactly the sort of summer cottage you'd pick for a Labor Day weekend, but we made the best of it. Under my directions she filled the pails with me holding the light. Then we made a triumphant charge out again. The horses were very large and eager out there and it certainly was dark. Pooh barked. I quickly laid out some verbal scheduling regarding the placement of pails and the quick return to the car while my sister, who doesn't play with words when there are sterner matters afoot, deposited the pails strategically, closed the barn door, and carried the bucket of grain for the goats under the fence to the car, where I was already revving the engine. I gestured wildly with the flashlight in appreciation. Working together this way we were an unbeatable team. Pooh seemed to agree.

We drove the few yards to the goats' corral. The expectant ecstasy with which they greeted us was very moving, in fact it almost knocked us over. We were in the groove now, each confident in her role. I held the light and shouted. My sister undid the gate, took in the pail, filled the pans, patted the goats, returned and closed the gate, and the job was done.

Nothing to it really. It was nice to know we could do an unaccustomed job so well, be relied on and dependable. I, for one, felt fulfilled. Next time I'm going to try it with my hands tied behind my back, and I bet I do just as good a job that way too.

The Unhappy Hunting Ground

When you set out in the morning chill
and stalk near the brow of the tawny hill,
lean and hungry and out to kill,
a stir in the bush! A rustle!—Will
you chance to think with a sudden thrill
that it might be a deer? Of course! A shot!—
Will you stop to think that it just might not?
The thought is cold when the blood runs hot!
My dog is large and the color of fawn,
and blood runs high in the early dawn.
My children have jackets of tan and dun,
and sport is sporting, and fun is fun
as the hunter stalks where the deer may run,
but I've got a bead on the hapless one
that comes THIS way with a loaded gun!

Turn To Chapter VI, Please

I was substituting as biology teacher at Sea Pines School the other day, a role in which I am a tragic figure of fun. We had riffled through the pages of Chapter V as a gesture toward reviewing for a test. My voice was droning plaintively through the pall of torpor it cast over the room, when, on turning the page, I jerked back in awe and wonder. Chapter VI was upside down.

I was elated. I don't know when I've felt so refreshed. Not wanting to disturb this remarkable book, I moved from the south side of the desk around to the north and looked at it again. The words were no longer diving, but they still looked uncomfortably displaced, and I soon realized that the whole chapter was backside-to as well. In other words, from the southern point of view, page 56 at the end of Chapter V was followed by page 73 of Chapter VI (upside-down) whose pages then went 72, 71, 70...and so on down to 57, which was followed by page 74 at the beginning of Chapter VII (upside-up). I became so excited over this, and my mind was so filled with the symbolic and philosophical significance of it all, that I immediately turned the class over to an alert, scientifically-oriented student with a conformist biology book and withdrew into a corner with my thoughts.

There may be political symbolism here, concerning the North and the South and biology and civil rights, but this didn't occur to me until much later. At the time I pictured huge stacks of biology books being packaged in cartons at the publishing house, each volume a clean, crisp, identical replica of its siblings. I pictured our vast factories of secondary school education dealing out these uniform textbooks to symmetrical rows of docile students, and saw thousands of pupils plodding dutifully from Chapter I to the end of the book without once having to move around the desk or swivel the book to get at Chapter VI. Yet here was I with this unique treasure, perhaps the only biology book of its kind in the world. Who else could claim a Chapter VI moving backward on its head in an otherwise functional bio book? I chose to imagine that I was the only one, and the concept made me feel festive and singled-out. If a postage stamp printed with a flaw is a priceless find to a stamp collector, shouldn't a book with an eccentric chapter be a prize to a book collector? It should, but is it? No. Not often, anyway. Then why did it delight me so? It could not bring me riches and recognition. It couldn't even bring me better biology. All I had, really, was a rather dull book with a deformity.

Yet, for one thing, when a regiment marches by or a chorus-line dances there is something very exciting about spotting one of the performers out of step. The mere fact of being different, even in an unconstructive way, relieves the monotony. It is a beauty spot of diversity standing out against the smooth cheek of perfection.

But I think the real answer lies in my reaction toward the book's personality. Books are as irritating or enchanting as people. Sometimes they are even annoying because you can't talk back to them. To me this particular book was dry, factual, smug and authoritarian. It was well-organized and businesslike. It was cold, precise and rational. It left little to the imagination, and ignored the poetic aspects of its subject. It talked down to me as though I were a hopeless clod. As I read it I kept wanting to poke it in the ribs or hold out my foot to trip it up. Then along came Chapter VI, clowning around in that ludicrous position, and all my antagonism left me. The book was human after all. It was fallible. It didn't always know which end was up, any more than you or I. It even had a sense of humor in a crude sort of way. Through its guileless discard of dignity it became my friend. It lowered itself to my level. We were tragic figures of fun together.

Of course not everyone feels the same way about a personality. The regular science teacher was back on the job the next day, and since the book was really his, not mine, I had to leave it in his care, though I thought of it often. In a way it haunted me. After a few days went by I asked after it, and he said,

"Oh that—I turned it in for a good one."

—

Beatle-browed

One of the fringe benefits of teaching is the window it opens into the hearts of childhood, or in our case at Sea Pines School, female youthhood. Here we may glance through magic casements opening on gardens of awakened awareness flowering with the hopes and fears of future years. Let us lean our elbows on the window sill and look more closely. Four hairy Beatles glare back. Four un-American millionaires are bobbing up and down in the hearts of our studentry saying they want to hold their hands. Never were hands more willing, moist and warm. Never were voices more shrill in exultation. Last week, this week and next mark the invasion victory of the Beatles of Britain over United States teenagery, and our little corner of East Brewster is not the least of those trampled prostrate.

The Beatles are four energetic guitar playing vocalists who wear their hair in the cloche style usually associated with Joan of Arc, and sing in pseudo-American pop accents that defeat description and their British heritage. Cool is the adjective the girls use for them in calmer moments. They jog around convulsively as they render their selections, which are accompanied by an orchestration of female shrieks from the audience. Their hair flops over their faces in time with the mad tempo, providing the Beatle-browed look.

What does all this mean to us at Sea Pines, where we may possibly represent a microcosm of a country faced with a very real problem? It means we called a special faculty meeting before last Sunday's Ed Sullivan show on Channel 5, to decide whether we would try to beat the Beatles or join them. There was little argument and no choice. We rearranged the study hall hours on B-Day so that H-Hour from 8-9 pm would be free, and retired to our sound-proof chairs.

I couldn't stay in mine, though. I emerged into the living room and crept stealthily toward the T.V., tempted as Eve for a bite of the diabolical apple of knowledge. Seven miles insulated me from the din in East Brewster, but the studio audience gave me the pitch. I was determined to be a girl again, and find out if I could feel like squealing. What I saw surprised me. I expected the noise, and the jumping about and the hair and guitars, but behind or beneath it all the Beatles looked old. To me their faces looked drawn and care-worn. And why not, I thought. With millions of dollars to take care of, millions of husky girls ready to smother them, what did they have to be young about? What does the future hold for them? More money, more police protection. Maybe some day they'll be urged to run for parliament. I couldn't bring myself to squeal for them and felt almost melancholy as I switched off the set.

The telephone rang. "Did you see them, Mrs. Cochran? Aren't they cool!"

"Sure they're cool, but they looked old to me, much older than I thought they were."

"What did you expect? They're all around twenty-five!"

"Well, I'll write my column about them, anyway."

"Of course, what else is there to write about?"

Without Naming Names

Everyone admits to forgetting names now and then. One can always find a sympathetic ear for one's accounts of staggering faux pas, whenever one's name-dropping has meant dropping clear out of sight. I have several such stories that will top yours any day, including the one about trying to introduce my fiancé to my dinner hostess and drawing a blank on both counts.

But what used to be rare enough occasions to be given the "wait'll-you-hear-this" treatment have suddenly become daily routine. For what more vulnerable position could there be for name problems than that of a new headmaster's wife, in charge of admissions. With names clustered around me, jostling and shoving, standing between me and clear thinking, between me and insight, between me and hope, never a day goes by that I don't forget a dozen or more, and some days they come over the plate so fast I can't even swing at them.

So I have decided at last that it is more just to everyone if I stop trying completely. Assuming a fey and vacuous air, my face seraphic in its innocence, I henceforth scatter my meaningless little thoughts like Ophelia's flowers at the feet of unnamed multitudes, leaving the introductions up to fate.

Thus it is possible, I have found, to go through a whole afternoon of parents' reception at Sea Pines School without naming any names at all. Of course there are various ruses that help—bits of subterfuge to hide behind. To the question, "Do you remember me?" you say courteously, "Of course," and move on. To, "How is my daughter doing?" you say, 'Fine," and if they look surprised, add "—considering." "Did you drive all the way today?" you ask conversationally (hoping they don't live in Sandwich), and during lulls you interject, "So good of you to come all this way...Have you seen the new dorm?...Get someone to show you through the lab...Now please be sure to sign the guest book—we like to keep a record...Why don't you talk to her teachers? It's probably a matter of her finding herself and developing good study habits...So good of you to come all this way..."

But there can be pitfalls—

"You say you would like a motel reservation? Well now let's see —my-uh-secretary-uh-just a minute—will it be in your name?— Uh, yes of course—uh—Oh," (passing the buck) "There you are dear...By the way, you people do know my husband of course, don't you?"

"Of course," says your husband courteously, moving on. Later, in the privacy of the boudoir, he says, "Why didn't you introduce me to the Fartherfields? You were talking to them for hours, I hear, and I really wanted to meet them."

You look at him fatuously.

"I couldn't remember your name, dear," you say.

Towers of Strength

Towers of strength among women come, I've decided, every other generation. My mother is and always was a tower of strength. She will say, "Oh, Betsy—really!" when she reads this, but she can't deny that she has always made the best plans, and put them through more efficiently and gracefully than anyone I know. She is equal to and makes the best of every situation. One naturally falls in step behind her, docile and admiring. As a child I assumed that this was the way mothers always were—that some day it would be my turn. It would be I, some day, who would usher wide-eyed daughters to New York, opening the doors to the wonders of cosmopolitan culture. Being a mother, I would be able to turn the golden keys smoothly, as mothers should.

A score of years has passed since I became a mother, but it hasn't taught me a thing about turning keys. I still have to hunt for them first—dumping everything out of my handbag onto the floor, and sifting through it trembling. Ah, here we are—found at last. Which way up does it go? Why doesn't it fit? Which way does it turn? I hear a voice behind me—"Oh really, mother! Let me try."

I took my youngest daughter to New York last weekend, determined to open some doors for her. In preparation for my role as mistress of ceremonies, I laid a few ground rules—she was to wear stockings and pumps, for example, rather than knee socks and sneakers—and I suggested that we visit museums, see a Broadway play and perhaps a movie at Radio City Music Hall, tour the New York Times (because I wanted to), do a little shopping and so on.

I should have saved my breath. She was a tower of strength and a pillar of purpose from the moment we stepped off the plane. She went along with the stockings-and-pumps nonsense for a day and a half to please me, but after that I found we were both wearing sneakers and I was falling in step behind her, docile and admiring. We tramped through Greenwich Village bringing back some gummy French pastries to eat in our room in bed. We loped athletically through the Metropolitan Museum, and then went to the circus, getting there in plenty of time to visit the animals before the show.

The next day we went to the Central Park Zoo, allowing plenty of time to visit the animals, and ate a leisurely meal there surrounded by them, at the outdoor cafeteria. We squeezed in a play and movie, raced through the Frick Museum and the Cloisters some time during the weekend, and spent all of Sunday until we had to leave at the Bronx Zoo. She decided early in the game that it would save time if she took care of the room key, and she was the one who was always ready with the correct bus fare.

We never did tour the New York Times. She didn't really want to ("You go ahead mother, if you like") but happily for our relationship the tour offered was closed when I called. We covered a lot of mileage, saw mounds of humanity, found it lacking and sought out animals. I've never seen so many animals, even on a Disney film. But the zoos did nothing to raise mankind's score in my daughter's eyes. The cages were too bare. The animals were bored. Why couldn't they have more freedom and fun? I fell in step with her and agreed. The crowning touch was the discovery that almost all the greenery and flowers in the bird cages were plastic. At the Bronx Zoo there is a large sign in red lettering saying, "The Most Destructive Animal in the World." Under it is a mirror. If we had stayed another day I think we would have spent it opening all the cages, hoping to restore the balance of nature.

We finally picked our way to the Elevated through the littered streets, past the vendors of huge pink balls of sticky air—spun sugar on a stick, and lurched downtown on the Lexington Avenue Express through what must be the largest most concentrated monument to human squalor ever built. My train left Grand Central before hers. "Have you got everything? Will you be all right?" I asked lamely, knowing she had and would. She was planning to while the time away at a Disney animal film shown at the station theatre, but she insisted on seeing me safely aboard my train and comfortably settled first. She said goodbye as an affectionate dutiful daughter should, but her expression, if I can read expressions, said, "Have you got everything? Will you be all right?"

Granny Gives Birth

Boss: It's been almost a month since I have written, but I have been very busy giving birth to my first grandchild—no paltry feat, sir. Grandmother and granddaughter doing well, thank you. Congratulations are in good order...statistically speaking for all 22 inches, eight pounds one ounce of Maria ("say it loud and there's music playing; say it soft and it's almost like praying")...artistically speaking for the flawless assembling of navy blue eyes in a rose and peach setting with a form to outshine the most idealistic dream of a classic Greek or Italian Renaissance Master...sentimentally speaking for the aura of perfection down to the smallest toenail. Ah, me.

It isn't everyone who can be a grandmother. You, for instance, are a loser in this department, boss, and always will be. More than the advantages of sex, however, is the display of technique and talent that goes into this sort of undertaking. One must be firm of character and opinion, agile of limb and possessed of dominating genes (to ascertain that the baby will look like members of *your* family). Then a procedural pattern must be followed that goes something like this.

A mother, who must be your daughter or daughter-in-law and will hereafter be referred to as the Delivery Agent or D.A., discloses her blessed condition early in the game, succumbing immediately to your ministerings and advice. You, as prospective grandmother (P.G.), harken to the call of duty and Take Over. If the D.A. is your daughter you arrange for the doctor, layette, hospital, convalescence, the naming of the child and the worrying and waiting. Her role is to acquiesce. If she is your daughter-in-law you describe your own obstetrical experiences in detail, dwelling on the arduous aspects of your labor, and fill her in on all the family traditions or prejudices surrounding such events.

At this stage you also go out and buy some size 1 and 2 aluminum needles and, having decided on a grandson, cast on sixty stitches of heather-blue wool. Over the next six or seven months you knit-one, purl-one whenever you are at the lunch club, as a conversation starter. "Why Betsy, you're not...?"

"Yes, I'm expecting a grandchild—in January!"

"Darling, why who would have guessed it—how simply marvelous!" etc.

When hard labor starts (as if it hadn't been going on right along) the revelation comes to you that there is no labor like the labor of a first-time grandmother. The vicarious abdominal contractions—the worry, the excitement—the giving the doctor a piece of your mind—the telephoning—the waiting, the pacing, the telling the D.A. what to pack—the emotional experience is overwhelming, boss, it really is. And I have had it and I want your word of admiration.

There is, though, one thing a grandmother doesn't have to do. She doesn't have to boil water. Water-boiling is for grandfathers. It keeps them busy and out of the way. I'm telling you this, for when your turn comes. . .

And so, march on, oh generations!

Granny, Snarled in the Internet, Snarls Back

You? Online?" they say, laughing raucously. "Why not?" I ask, knowing perfectly well why not. They think I'm too old.

Get lost, you digital dingbats! I've been speeding along Information Superhighways since before you were born, unless you're John Ullman.

Originally such trips probably started with hand signals, moving along to smoke signals, carrier pigeons, Marathon runners and Paul Revere. The pace picked up in the early 1900s when I was invented, and we tossed off dot 'n' dash telegrams, got mixed up in telephone party line partying, rolled with the radio rage, TVs and computers as they came along, and now this, so what's the big deal? You've had one communication revolution, you've had them all.

I remember as a child sitting on the floor with my crystal radio set attached to a bedspring, listening to a self-conscious announcer talking in a sing-song voice, and knowing I was experiencing a miracle. Far away voices coming through the air! No wires, no bullhorns!

Each new discovery was pure magic, but that was just to begin with. Later on they got to be old hat and no more miraculous than the rest of life. Some finally became undernourished and virtually obsolete.

Obsolescence has been stalking my computer ever since I finished paying for it. It went through a two-week siege of Black Screen Disease last month (just after I went on-line) that meant I had to unplug everything, heave it into the car and take it to a computer hospital in Hyannis where they tut-tutted over it and finally replaced a teensy-weensy battery I didn't even know it had. Since then, after struggling to get the plugs back in where they belong, and a slight-of-hand adjustment by Nate Knight of Knight Design in Orleans, I'm back to answering my backed-up e-mail and once more experiencing the ephemeral delights of cyberspace.

But here's the big catch: no matter how wide the Web or what speed communication travels, it's still 90 percent junk mail. It may get here a lot faster, but the ratio between trash and treasure stays the same. It's state-of-the-art and quicker than thought itself, but what have we gained? –Time.

Quality time? Time for what? Time to meditate, it's true, and a good idea. Time not to have to hunt for envelopes and stamps and go to the post office. Time not to spend hours in the library on research projects. But I like going to the post office; I love going to the library; these are almost the only people-friendly rituals we have left.

So the question isn't am I too old for the Internet, it's why bother?

I had a couple of good reasons for bothering. One of my greatest great nieces said yes, she'd love to come to the Cape for a weekend this summer but she'd like to be able to do something for us, and offered to put us Online. Well, if those were her terms, why not? So she tossed a serviceable, modestly-priced modem and a 538-page America Online guide into her car and came down and did it. (Hence my Online byline, which stands for Great Aunt Bets at America Online dot com. I forget what "com" means.)

Of course I'm too old to understand most of what she did, although her explanations were exquisite. But I'm delighted and not too old to have lured her down here to do it. (Being on the Cape helps; we'll take credit for that, too.)

Another reason for bothering was that many members of our extended family are on-line, and more inclined to communicate by e-mail than otherwise, since it's cheaper, quieter, quicker and more peaceful than the telephone. Once you're signed on, that is. But not more private.

I was never the right age to understand high tech stuff. I formed a close attachment to my typewriter in the old days, but never understood it, especially when it came to changing the ribbon. We accepted each other, as one learns to do with close attachments. I've been told you can never have a relationship of trust with a computer, so love and loyalty don't come into it. Remember, however enmeshed you become in the Internet, Black Screen Disease may strike any second.

There are other snide comments about computers and on-lining that suggest themselves. Why, for instance does computer technology use a whole lot of good old familiar words with entirely new meanings for them? Why, with cyberspace available, is the Internet so niggardly in its use of spaces, as in signatures, for example?

But to get back to content, "if it can't pass the 'so what?' test, throw it out" my writing teacher used to tell us 50 years ago. It's good advice still waiting to be acted on. It might be nice if all the time we're saving being on-line could be spent churning out deathless poetry and prose equal in quality to its racing speed. But then again...

So what?

FLOTSAM AND JETSAM

SECTION 2

Nourishment

Nourishment

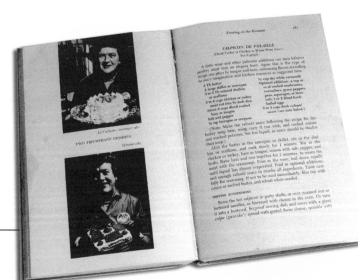

An Open Letter to the French Chef

Dear Julia Child: Many a long year has seen me salivating silently in front of TV, watching you as you did your "chose culinaire." Larding the airwaves with succulent wisdom and toothsome wit, you cavorted blithely through my Monday nights from puff pastry to the "filets de poisson poches au vin blanc," with me sitting paralyzed with admiration, helpless as a shore-stranded jellyfish. But last Saturday I changed my role, for a madcap whirl of hours.

My husband had gone to a sailing regatta, and the whole day stretched out full length, for me to squander as I saw fit. I saw fit to pay my bills at first, but because it was Saturday, I knew no one would appreciate the gesture until Monday, so since it was raining and I was hungry, I opened up *The French Chef* and plunged right up to my ears in savory Boeuf Bourguignon. For once in my life I read the directions and paid attention. Utter concentration. No short cuts. When you called for butter, I settled for nothing less than 94 score. When you said to mash garlic I mashed garlic instead of sneaking by with a few shakes of garlic powder. I induced lean, generous chunks of bottom of the round to simmer ever so gently in red wine, thyme, bay leaf and all, with the juices blending lusciously in their fire-proof casserole on a slow, slow burner. It was a nostril quivering excitement that built up in me as I concocted enough ambrosia for at least two meals. Overnight the juices would rest together in consummate bliss.

Around 5 pm my husband returned to find me still sweating over the hot stove. The meat had had its four hours and was now fork-tender. The flavors were whispering vows of eternal constancy and making the air astringent with their aromatic promises. I helped myself to a lip-smacking taste, added soupçon of salt, and prepared to pour the juice through a colander into another bowl to finish the sauce. But before I even touched it the casserole cracked. It was still on the burner. The crazed bottom then fell apart. Aghast, we saw the tide drop in the sea of bubbling nectar, and slowly seep through the burners into the bowels of the stove. Bleating in agony, I watched the meat deposited stark and naked on the bare burners.

The airy compliments that had hovered so near dissolved under the mopping up of the sponge. Once more heaven eluded me, but I haven't taken pen in hand to plea for your sympathy.

"You can still give the meat to the cats," said my husband, searching the ground for a crumb of comfort.

"We're going to eat this stuff if it kills us," I said. After plucking the visible pieces of glass out of the meat, I figured I could beef it up with another pint of red wine and bouillon (thyme, bay leaf, garlic, etc.). However, as I continued cleaning up, and went to remove the drip trays under the burners, they released a delicate stream of gravy which poured into another pan below. Picking up about four tbs. of dried flaky residue of spilled coffee and petrified black bean soup from previous overflowings, along with tiny grains of aluminum from a kettle that boiled out and melted last week, the juices had a new look. And if I do say so, after taking a deep breath, the taste was something you wouldn't believe. It was positively tongue-puckering, and sent tingles down my spine. It was—well—different, and while it might have sent some gourmets calling for dental floss or ipecac, I looked at it as an important variation on the theme, and felt you should know about it. I invited my daughter and her husband over and called up a neighbor whose wife had been away for a week so he was ready for anything, and after an hour or two of elbow-bending we had no serious trouble polishing the whole thing off. All the cats got were the plate scrapings, which they approached with what I felt was unnecessary caution.

Now I'm back at my old station in front of Channel 2, watching you peel asparagus butts. But I want you to know that for all the broken dreams, it was a peak experience, and I owe it all to you.

Bon apetit, vousmême,

B.C.

La Soupe de Poubelle Bouillie

Sometime in early January, as the still over-extended holiday family sits sullenly around the table waiting for the daily dietary dole-out, grandma, with a "Bon Appetit!" for all, comes up with her New Year's version of "la soupe de poubelle bouillie."

One of the beauties of "la soupe de poubelle bouillie" (or, as the kids call it, "poorbelly bully") is that it varies each year, and assembled relatives who have run out of inoffensive conversation at this stage in their visiting, can be as offensive as they like, reminiscing over former soups de p.b. compared with this one. (They are in favor of this one because they know it's all they're going to get before they set out on the long road home to Hackensack or Presque Isle or wherever. They won't know how they really feel about it until they've been driving for an hour or so and it has had a chance to fraternize with their vitals.)

Grandma enjoys these discussions; in fact she forgoes sulking in the kitchen to draw up a chair and listen. She likes the thought that she is constantly improving on the old family recipe and will go on improving on it each year until she is up stirring her great soup pot in the sky.

And it is an old family recipe. One of her forebears long ago brought it over turbulent seas from the old country, which in this case was the Island of Jersey. This French-speaking Channel Island belongs to Britain but was occupied by Germany during World War II, all of which brought about a cuisine that is at best eclectic. Compared with mainland French cooking it lacks that "je ne sais quoi," and the quoi the British add is best left on the side of the plate. But in that faraway day when grandma's forebear was engaged in a hand-to-mouth battle for survival, the recipe he tucked into the secret pocket of his doublet had little more to it than a French accent and a lot of possibilities that would, in the land of plenty overseas, take root, he hoped.

Of course, "la soupe de poubelle bouillie," translated literally, means, "the soup of garbage boiled," but, in practice, grandma does not translate it literally. She simmers it, rather than boils it, at a heat just high enough to threaten the life of any lurking bacteria hanging around with intent to kill. (Intent to maim is another thing and serves to build a hardier race, grandma says.)

Timing is important in making an outstanding poorbelly bully. Its ingredients are assembled throughout the holiday season after each meal, and although they used to be kept in crocks out in the shed mulling in vinegar and salt until festivities called for their final cooking, or were simmered steadily in huge vats on the back of the range throughout the 12 days of Christmas and then some, nowadays grandma freezes them. This means that when grandpa bellows from the kitchen as he is scraping the plates after a heavy meal, "Whaddaya want done with the plate scrapings, Maw? Into the soup kettle as usual?" she no longer hisses, "Don't you realize that recipe's supposed to be secret, Paw?" Now she just says, "bag 'em, Paw, and stick 'em in the freezer."

But the most important thing about the timing is that it be long enough to include samples from all those optimistic leftovers dishes that follow the roasts of turkey, beef and ham: the beef Creole and the turkey forshmak, the stuffed peppers, the goulash and the jambalaya, the shepherd's pie, the macaroni 'n' fixin's salad, the mixed minced meat hash and the overstuffed eggplant. Only then can a good honest "soupe de poubelle bouillie" deserve to be called mature, let alone ripe.

Then comes the final "boiling" which is generally done over a fire outdoors, weather and Town permitting, with the younger children gathering around to watch, giggling behind their face masks, while the rest of the family takes off for an early movie. In go two tablespoons of chili powder and two of curry powder per gallon. In go 10 twists of saffron and a scoop of wolfsbane; red pepper to taste.

After that there's nothing to it. Grandma ladles it into a colander or food mill, pressing through as much solid matter as possible. Sometimes she puts it through the blender, but not always, depending on whether she wants this year's p.b. smooth or crunchy. Then back on the fire with it for a few minutes, for a tasty tongue-scalding brew.

"Bong!" goes the dinner gong, and the rest is up to us.

Getting A Dressing Down

We are seven at table, or rather tables, since the waitress has had to push two together. She stands over us with moistened pencil. With no small sense of virtue and accomplishment we have each decided on an entree from the menu—fish, chicken, whatever, and picked our potato, mashed or fried. She is not impressed

"What kinda dressing?" she asks.

"Huh?"

"What kinda dressing on your salad?"

"Oh—what kinda dressing you got?"

"French, Italian, Thousand Island, House," says the waitress. She clearly anticipates our tedious deliberation. She knows we will shilly-shally.

My palms grow damp. I feel my turn coming before I'm ready. It's that word "dressing."

Dressing. Ambiguous enough as a verb ("Are you dressing for dinner or do we come as we are?"). As a noun, especially an international salad noun, it's frightening.

I have, at a less worldly time of life, said "French" when the question was poised, picturing a definitive olive oil combined with wine, tarragon, or simple cider vinegar, freshly-ground salt and pepper and a kiss of garlic, thrown together in friendship over lightly crisp green lettuce, as my good old basic cookbook said to do. When the iceberg wedges arrived besmeared with a viscous day-glo ointment I was disappointed.

To judge by what the supermarket has to offer among the internationals, Italian seems closer to the oil-and-vinegar formula among the prepared dressings, but let's see what we're really getting into: "partially hydrogenated soybean oil, water, white distilled vinegar, sugar, dried garlic, hydrolyzed vegetable protein, spices, xanthan gum (improves mixing), oxstearin (prevents cloudiness under refrigeration), calcium disodium EDTA (protects flavor), artificial color." The list grows parenthetically defensive as it goes along.

Why add water, when all the water has just been carefully patted off the leaves? Why xanthan gum (which I just bet could wipe out a colony of laboratory rats) to improve mixing? Oil and vinegar aren't supposed to mix. Complement each other, yes—even fraternize, but mix, no. And what's the matter with cloudiness under refrigeration? Who wouldn't be cloudy under refrigeration?

I want to be madly in love with a flavor before I put up with calcium disodium EDTA added to protect it. (Another candidate to destroy the flavor of life for experimental animals?) Then we come to "artificial color." Italian dressing is dishwater color. Was this done artificially? What was it beforehand that made this necessary? At home one doesn't need to fake dishwater color of the salad dressing. A simple oil-and-vinegar emulsion with plenty of pepper and salt does the trick with no help at all.

"You want me to come back when you've made up your mind?" the waitress queries pointedly.

"Yes." But I feel her hovering. Thousand Island. Now we're in very deep. The Thousand Islands, lying as they do between New York and Ontario, have every right to be ambivalent, culinarily; we shouldn't look for singlemindedness in one of their recipes. Sure enough, Irma Rombauer in her *Joy of Cooking* takes us the mayonnaise and catsup route. Only the debris added (olives, green pepper, chopped egg) distinguishes it from Russian dressing. (No doubt this is all a Russian plot.) Fanny Farmer, on the other hand, apparently frequents a different Thousand Island. She wants us to mix orange and lemon juice, paprika, salt, onion juice, mustard and stuffed olives with olive oil, and chill.

There may be a thousand other versions from the other Thousand Islands.

This leaves "House." "House" could mean anything. What the dressing business needs is a good zoning code.

"Don't you have any Roquefort?" I suggest as if changing the subject, when she comes back.

"Blue cheese is thirty cents extra," she says, writing it down quickly and firmly. Her making the decision is worth every penny.

Fat Of The Land

We've known several cats that went wild here on the Cape, not because they were underfed or deserted. If anything they were bored with the tidbits fed them from packages or can and chose to get their own, stalking, hunting, living off mice, moles and minnows and finding perfect protection in the heavy under- growth.

We've know several people that went wild here too, periodically at any rate, and we think it's natural—it's that kind of place. It comes of knowing you can live off the fat of the land.

Most of us live financially off the fat of the tourist trade, but spiritually, and sometimes literally, always joyfully, many of us live off the fat of the land rolling in wealth.

Our vegetation may not seem lush, but when fall comes we gather in a harvest that we would not swap for all the orange groves in California. (Anyway, our new cook book tells us that rose hips, and we have plenty of rose hips, contain 900% more vitamin C than orange juice, so there). We have cranberries hanging like clusters of rubies even in the abandoned bogs in such profusion that you have to be careful not to crush them underfoot. We have tangy wild grapes, and (every other year or so) beach plums whose elixir we jell and store. There are apple and pear trees where the old farms used to be, and in Eastham, turnips. Blueberries have gone by, but their memory lingers in jar and freezer, as may that of wild asparagus, strawberries, blackberries. Mushrooms take a little knowing, but we have them, both toothsome and toxic.

And off shore during scallop season all you need is a license and a pair of waders and you may stoop and scoop in your bushel. Oysters R tasty, -clams, mussels, quahogs make good chow in chowder, or raw, or steamed. Fish, so many kinds, are right out there where the other fellow is casting. Ducks, geese, upland fowl, deer and rabbits may be stalked in season, if you can bear to shoot them.

But it isn't just in the eating that's the proof of the pudding, here. It's in the getting. If you haven't rowed out to a sand bar in clear, crisp October weather to pluck scallops off the floor of the bay, or awaited the chilly dawn in a duck blind, a dawn whose first rays put every sunset you ever saw to shame—if you haven't cast into the surf alone on a beach that stretched out on either side of you until it disappeared in the curve of the earth, or filled your pockets with gleanings from a russet cranberry bog in Indian summer; if you haven't gathered the harvest you haven't lived off the fat of the land. For it's the taking part in the culling of the fill that makes it really living. The fitting survival of the fittest.

Cranberry Carol

Sing the cranberry, as September lengthens! As the bogs begin to purple, it's time for scoop and box. Even the half-forgotten bog that hasn't been worked for years tempts neighboring housewives to put on old jeans, grab a basket, and set off for the Lilliput jungle to garner the harvest.

Cranberrying has an appeal of its own, not to be compared with beach plumming, graping, appling or gathering in of pumpkin. It has its unique joys and hazards. Through the tall dry grass you pick your way gingerly, wary of catbriar, vagrant rosebush and black snake, until, one step further and you are in the ditch. No, no, you catch yourself just in time where the grass arches slightly toward your temptation, teeter on the brink wondering how lusty a leap is required of the arthritic joints, make the plunge and land shaky but triumphant in your little Eden.

Watch out now. You don't want to step on them. Flecks of ruby spark the heather tweed colors underfoot, and here and there the bullfight red challenge of poison ivy flashes. Pity poor Eve, in the thrall of such display!

The nice thing about cranberry picking is that you can sit down while working—that is, if you're a hand-picker. It's not easy on the back, if the back is thirty-five years parted from the last game of jack-stones, but it gives the legs a rest, and you can always vary your position by kneeling for a spell, or even lying on your stomach if you don't mind prickles. As you peer under the motherly foliage, wondering if there's a good crop this year, there are the teardrop jewels, hanging in shy perfection.

Short of horse-chestnuts, what are more satisfactory than cranberries for beauty and touch? If they had no other excuse for being, this would be enough. Color, shape, texture—the sound they make when they bump together—all just right.

But they have so many other excuses. Juice, sauce, jelly, pie, relish, marmalade, bread, even pancakes are the better for them. No pits or stones to clog the drain—no peeling or coring to do. They awaken the palate and are kind to the kidney!

So you scoop them home from your local grocer, or stop by the self-service roadside stand to insert your quarter in the top of the glass jar and pick up a bag of them. Or better far, go and sit among them in an uncivilized bog, exposed to sea wind, feeling the lick of poison ivy leaf across erring knuckles, hearing the faint rustle of field-mouse or black snake in the grass nearby, gathering in and singing the cranberry in the grateful, hungry, lonesome tones of autumn—until at last you creak to your feet, lumber cautiously back over the ditch, and make for home, laden with peerless loot.

Two in the Bush

It was a gentle afternoon;
A mocha tint caressed the dune;
The hue in thicket and in grove
could almost be described as mauve,
which indicated with asurety
Beachplums had attained maturity.

We sauntered out with gun on shoulder,
Light of heart, and thought no bolder
than to quaff the local view
and maybe down a crow or two.
(now Madden, turn your eye of eagle!
Shooting crows is strictly legal!)

Hardly had we gained the knoll
when something checked our placid stroll—
two ladies, past life's early Spring—
two gentlewomen, trespassing!
And worse, Oh far far worse to tell
a-foraging for fruit as well!

They turned, the wicked thieving pair!
They turned and met our baleful stare.
They saw us armed and steely-eyed.
They flinched. They blanched. As one, they cried,
"Take half! Take all our beachplums, but
don't shoot!" We shook our heads. Tut, tut!

Ah, never was a sight so sorry.
Ladies, you were not our quarry!
Let the sin of Eve persist;
a plum or two will not be missed.
But let it now occur to you
why God made poison ivy too!

The Call Of The Beachplum

One bright carefree day in July my husband stopped me in the driveway and said, "Come here, I want to show you something." Right away I knew there was something wrong. There was a challenging timbre to his voice that told me I was going to be expected to do something. He led me to a beachplum bush. Every twig on it was covered with ominous little green lumps. They were as thick as fruit flies around a jelly bag.

"Gonna be a bonanza year," he said, leering meaningfully.

"Oh, you never know," I replied with a brave shrug. But there was an icy chill around my heart.

That was six weeks ago. It wasn't a bad summer, all told. I thought the drought in late July and early August might have done in the green lumps, and in truth they didn't seem to be getting any bigger, but a friend whose bushes were similarly afflicted pointed out, "They're not falling off."

They never did fall off. I have to report that I just checked them, and they are plumping out and changing color, gearing up for the plucking. By the time I finish writing about it they'll be dead ripe.

There go the two best weeks in the year. And, come to think of it, there may not be that many years left. With every year that goes by, there's one less year to look forward to, and this means two less weeks in early September.

But to those who hear it, the beachplum's song is a siren's song. Try to ignore the clarion call into the bush—block it out of your mind—drive down town, do something else. Rev up your motor, close your eyes, and gun it right by those bushes. All in vain.

No matter that you don't even like beachplum jelly—that you know it's 50 percent sugar—poison full of empty calories. No matter that a good many friends you'd like to give it to for Christmas don't like it either, because of the heavy, heady flavor and cloying aftertaste. Greed, vigorous, driving, irrational greed spurs you on. A siren's song is a siren's song, and when you've got to go you've got to go.

Besides, jelly isn't the only way of disposing of the processing problem. There's beachplum-vodka liqueur. There's jam. According to Euell Gibbon who loved to stalk the wild recipe, there's beachplum chiffon pie. There are experiments for the making. Try spraying some of the more colorful beachplums with urethane and piling them on a glass dish for a centerpiece. They'll look as pretty as hard candy, and you won't try eating them more than once.

Beachplumming means total immersion, when you get into it, of you, your life, and your kitchen. Everyday doings like eating, answering the telephone, going shopping, paying bills, become irrelevant. Social give-and-take grinds to a halt.

You cancel all appointments, put the phone on two-week hold, send the kids off to stay with Granny. You get a good night's sleep before taking the plunge to brave the rigors of the hunt. If you have a choice you pick a cool, cloudy, windy day, so you can wear stiff jeans and a windbreaker against scratches and poison ivy, without dying of the heat or having to wear a hat. If the going is swampy where you're headed, the best footgear is rubber boots.

If you're a real professional with more than four or five accessible bushes to service you, you favor equipment like that of the Flathead Lake cherry pickers of Montana—reversed backpack straps tied together at the back, supporting a plastic bucket in front at about the beltline. But for jungle areas the basket with handle is more maneuverable, and you're less likely to be trapped among thorns. It should be wide-based enough not to tip easily, and with it you take a plastic cup to hold in one hand while you pick into it with the other. The basket collects the base supply. Try not to step in it.

The addict has a mental map of an area's productive bushes, however remote, permanently etched from previous forays. Yellow bushes are likely to ripen first, then red, then purple, and piebald last—but don't count on it. Regular checks should be made during ripening season.

Home equipment: Plenty of bags of sugar bought before the rush is on. There's no real substitute for sugar in beachplum jelly, so a beachplum aficionado must ignore the supermarket plea to restrain buying while the price is high. Old discarded nylon marquisette curtain material for jelly bags. Paraffin in a metal pitcher good for pouring, that can be put on the stove. Jars. Lids. Purists eschew commercial pectin and gather wild apples instead.

Finally: a good comfortable bed at the finish.

So it goes, for the fortnight ahead, and we must knock off and be up and at it.

Then when the last beachplum is picked, the siren song of the wild grape begins its seductive melody.

—●

Crabs

*In the shallowest of waters
on the wet and weedy sand
undetermined in their quarters,
whether sea or whether land*

*live the leggy loose crustaceans
long of limb and short of face
in their whims and affectations
not unlike the human race.*

*First the "horseshoe" prim and modest
not a crab in "crabbed" sense,
huge and heavy-skirted goddess
sailing on without defense.*

*Then the "sideways", sly and grabby
eyes that bulge and claws that crack
and the "hermit," slim and shabby
housed in some abandoned shack.*

*And their soft, seductive sister
sensitive of mien and shell
appetite cannot resist her,
dainty in chartreuse pastel.
On they scuttle till their travels
end on hook or salad plate.
As this rhapsody unravels
was it something that I ate?*

Feminine Angle

A ngling is at least half as instinctive to man as tail-chasing to a kitten. Spring—sap flowing—a stir in the lakes, streams and bay, and in the heart of man. Both the instinct to provide and the instinct of the chase take over.

So much for man, but how about woman? Quite a few women like to fish too. There are the glamorous surf-casters, the party-boat reelers, the aloof trout-stream type, and so on. It is a proud crowd, on the whole, that wears its hip-boots high. But there is another kettle of fisherwomen—flounder floozies—whose approach to the art of angling has its own languid charm.

Flounder fishing is a natural for amateurs and working women. You don't need much equipment, and what you need is cheap. A handline with hook and sinker (50¢) (extra hooks, 35¢) baited with a seaworm or the succulent belly of a clam, may bring you fillets fit for the most fastidious gourmet. You also need a wharf, prom-ontory, or small rowboat (borrowed) from which to dangle the line. You need patience and philosophy and can sometimes put up with the sluggish conversation of an equally sunstruck friend.

The procedure is simple but exacting. You take a late spring day like today, that dawns foggy, with the mist burning off at 11 am. At noon you tell the boss that—no, it's better just to take off muttering something about lunch and an appointment. You throw on a salty old pair of shorts and a sweatshirt, and run down to the beach where, if the tide is providentially low, you may be able to dig some bait, lacerating your fingers and tearing your nails. With this and your fishlines, a knife and pail, you are ready to shove off in the leaky pram.

Together you and your friend heave-ho the pram down to the water's edge. You row, while she bails. The sun smiles benignly as you maneuver for the spot near the bar where the flounder are sure to be hook-hungry. Anchor and lines go overboard and you stretch out your legs to get tan, and review the town gossip. A juicy ac-count is interrupted by a tug and up comes an eel, squirming and sliming up the line. Some may advocate grasping it and removing the hook. Another method is easier, quicker and less repulsive. That handy little knife finds a hundred uses.

Innumerable crabs and occasional sea robins and skate may submit to the hook before you give up. And now and then, to provide a balance, you haul up a flounder, a nice fat flatty looking like a close-mouthed politician with both eyes on one side of the issue.

What a delightful fish. No big gaping mouth. No spines or slime. Easy to clean and skin. Zip, zip, zip, zip, and rip and she's ready to be sautéed for breakfast, the heavenly reward for an afternoon well spent.

Throw Junior in the playpen—escape from tyrannical housework and office and come fishing! It is nature's tranquillizer and provides sole and solace for body and soul.

So long, boss!—Out for lunch and an urgent appointment...

Cape Cod Soliloquies

Cape Cod Soliloquies

Pleasant Bay, Narrows, South Orleans, Mass.

Shaping Up for the Season

If you think of the Cape as an arm in position for Indian wrestling, then the fingers are beginning to flex (around Provincetown) and the muscles are being toned for the Season's coming bout. But what the Cape Codders learned about wrestling from the gentle Nauset is pat-a-cake beside the tactics of the tourist game.

If you think of the Cape as a horn of seasonal plenty, open at the Canal end, hungry for another Season's bounty, then you may observe that it is now glistening with Spring beauty, and already receiving tasty tidbits on weekends.

If you think of the Cape as a codfish in the role of a toreador, luring the poor bull-headed tourist with his flashy Cape, then you have an overactive imagination, and are in danger of mixing matadors, or metaphors.

Let us consider instead that it is a genial crocodile, with his tail curling up to Provincetown, and his open jaws representing the Sagamore and Bourne bridges. His belly is red, white and blue for the National Seashore, and his back is, of course, a rich greenback green. He is rousing from his winter torpor and beginning to breathe fire. And that, O Best Beloved, means the Season is open, and tourists are beginning to run. He smells the blood of a New Jersey housewife.

As Lewis Carroll almost put it:

> *How doth the little crocodile*
> *Improve his shining tail*
> *And pour the surf of Nauset Beach*
> *On every golden scale!*
> *How cheerfully he seems to grin,*
> *How neatly spreads his claws,*
> *And welcomes little tourists in*
> *With gentle smiling jaws!*

Dead End

We had shaken out the rugs the other day and were slapping hornets with a fly swatter when up drove a car with strangers from some less favored state.

"Dead end," we called crisply out the window, landing a bullseye on a wasp.

"We were just driving around," said the mainlanders pleasantly.

We unbent a little. "Help yourselves," we said, reminding ourself that the booming economy of Cape Cod is utterly dependent on the tourist trade, and we are utterly dependent on the booming economy of Cape Cod. But we reflected a little bitterly that here it is barely spring, the season when daffodils are being flattened by northeast storms. Whether or not spring on the Cape is your dish of chowder, it bears no resemblance to summer, so what's going on here anyway? It's one thing that, with gracious condescension, we lend our beaches in summer, and quite another to have our spring reverie invaded. The great American summer (we viciously belted two hornets with one blow) starts July 4 and winds up with Labor Day, and any attempt to alter it is UnAmerican, or worse, UnCapeCod.

Smug and self-satisfied, we assumed a determined mien and gazed out the window over the bay, our bay. It's ours, all ours, we thought defensively. A flock of hooded mergansers scudded through the Narrows, and the hawk that has been hanging around for days banked gracefully above the trees. Our ducks, we whimpered inwardly—our hawk. We must keep Cape Cod safe for Cape Codders. Isolationism, that's what we need more of. Let's blow up the bridges and weigh anchor and drift ten miles east and secede.

Suddenly we remembered with panic that when it came to seceding we would never in the world pass for a Cape Codder. Holy mackerel, we haven't been here year 'round for a generation yet, and it is well within the memory of our older children when we ourselves were summer people. When the grand old tattered fishnet ensign is hoisted on Scargo Hill we'd be among the first to be dumped in the Canal.

We flinched guiltily, too, as we recalled how friendly everyone had been when we first moved down. The only ones who regarded us with suspicion were those who like us had recently moved in. Nobody tried to send us back. Nobody shouted "Dead end" at us.

Still there is such a thing as overcrowding. We took up the swatter again, but held it a moment to glance out at the unspoiled acres to the south and north, the wide wild beach to the east. Well, we're luckier than most. Some people are getting very crowded. Some other towns don't even have zoning, and you never know what will pop up in front of you or in back. The town owns part of what we can see, and that's good. The rest, except for our lot, is owned by summer people—summer people who have left the land almost as they found it, except for putting up a house and perhaps a boathouse, and clearing out a bit here and there.

So who are we to bite the hand that feeds us? Morons. And who are we to try to grapple with problems that properly belong to park commissions? Paranoids. Slightly distrait from all this mental turmoil we gazed vacantly at the ceiling and unwillingly found our eyes focusing on a whole army of hornets advancing from a crack between the beam and the chimney.

Ah, who indeed are we to play the great exterminator? We grabbed a squirt gun and sealed ourself off in our bedroom and haven't come out since, and don't plan to, not for a while.

Goosey Loosey

Fat sleek goose so long of neck,
swooping down with wings so
supple,
Are you lately from Quebec?
Did you see the Royal Couple?

Did you skirt the Rockbound Coast?
Navigate the inland route?
Linger, while we drink your toast!
Hear our twenty-gun salute!

Bird so suave and swift and cunning,
still unscratched, we know not how,
waterfowl, inured to gunning,
you would make a royal chow!

Six A.M. comes up like thunder
out of blinds across the bay,
while you honk in idle wonder,
and in pity, glide away.

Night and Day Crawlers

As inevitable as Spring and the robin come the night crawlers and the day crawlers. "Night Crawlers," advertised by the side of a country road, squirm deliciously in the minds of passing anglers, but for me they signal a flashback to childhood fantasy. What is a night crawler? A crawler by night, dummy. Wide awake we lie, in the dark of night and youth, sensing them under the bed, their thirteen legs wiggling, their antennae a-quiver, their bodies soft and spongy to the touch. They are creeping up the blankets, brushing tentacles across our face. They are scuttering in and out of the closet. They are swinging from the curtains by one claw. They scratch and whimper in the corners. They hide in bedroom slippers. They are nocturnal secrets of childhood not to be denied. Now that we are grown up we know that they are not real, of course. Now we can tell them to go away. Now, when we see the sign, "Night Crawlers," we can say, "Just another sign of Spring—time to go fishing," and drive on.

We won't drive on very fast though, because of the day crawlers. Day crawlers are more of a Cape Cod phenomenon. They too are seasonal, and Spring's the time for them, especially weekends. They are in the car in front of us—the man at the wheel with a map balanced on his knee—the woman looking out of the window, saying, "Look, Bertram, that's the house I was telling you about." They want to settle on the Cape, and that's just what they're doing, right in the middle of 6A and 28. They may never have gone below seventy all the way from New Jersey, they may be demons at the lane-shifting game on the Southeast Expressway, but since crossing the Canal they haven't once shifted out of low gear. Two steps forward and one back is the way their car cruises along. They love the Cape. You can tell. They want to savor every inch of it from a center-of-the-road position that will afford equal opportunity to both sides.

As we drive along behind them, again we lapse into our fantasy world. We picture parking the car and jogging along beside them, pointing out spots of local interest, or asking if they need help to get their car going. We picture shooting a long pole out from the top of our car across the top of theirs with signs that would hang down in front of the driver: "Get a Horse!" "Where's the Funeral?" "Pull on the emergency brake, your wheels are rolling!" "No Loitering!" And so on.

But it's nice to have Spring, whatever sort of crawlers come creeping.

Fishing Lanes

City-sickened, panting for the sticks,
they seek Rtes 3 and 28 and 6,
like lemmings lured and longing for the sea
beyond Rtes 28 and 6 and 3.
We cast our nets—throw out our hooks and bait
along Rtes 3 and 6 and 28.

Going to the Beach (Minority Opinion of One)

Iremember as a child of three being overcome by the smell of honeysuckle and wild roses as I was lumbering up the steep steps from the beach. It's that way again this year. You can't come by such bushes without being overwhelmed. What a year for Cape roses and honeysuckle!

It was the coming up that was especially significant to me. Coming up was a relief and comfort. Going down was another story and meant danger and treachery. Roses were prickly then, if I could notice them at all, and the sweetness of honeysuckle was as phoney as the stories everyone had told me about what fun it was going to be.

"You'll just love it," they said. "You'll love playing in the sand and paddling in the water."

Then they went down with me and sat in the shade of an umbrella reading a book, and my sister and I were told to go off and play. I felt hot and fat in my bathingsuit. The sun was zizzy and I wanted to be sick. The sand was sticky and the water was cold and the pebbles hurt. I hated it. I also knew that I wasn't measuring up to what was expected of me. Other kids went off and played happily. They built sand castles and went wading out too deep, and climbed in and out of the rowboats. I wanted to huddle under an umbrella by myself and freak out until it was time to go home. Other kids cried when they had to go up but not I. I couldn't wait to get home for supper, and I would eat too much to compensate for my inadequacy on the beach and feel fatter than ever the next day. The honeysuckle and rose memory as I was lumbering up the steps is the only good one I have of that period in my life.

Later on of course I learned to swim (though it took some doing) and finally managed to sidetrack my beach antipathy by developing a mania for hopscotch. To this day I can play a good solid game of hopscotch, and in my heyday I would take on all comers. I used to practice long hours on the wet sand of the ebbing tide to insure retaining my title. Somewhere within me I knew this was just a ploy to help me through the beach months of summer, but it worked and I was grateful.

Then I grew up and didn't have to go to the beach anymore unless I wanted to, so I hardly ever did. Once or twice I was trapped into going down with a group during a houseparty, for a swim and that sort of thing. It was the same old story. Sticky sand, Cold water, Zizzy sun. I sometimes would dig a clam or two with my bare hands to show I knew how, but nobody cared very much, and I tore my nails and the clams lay limp with their heads extended reproachfully until I dropped them back into their watery holes.

But beachgoing is a deathless ritual. One has to bring one's children to the beach, and so, dutifully, did I. They loved it. They went off and played. They built sand castles and waded and ran over the pebbles to make their feet tough. They skipped stones and made boats and rafts out of all sorts of things, and waded out too deep, and climbed in and out of rowboats.

It was no surprise to me to encounter the same old sticky sand and chilly waters. I showed the children how to dig clams with bare hands, and they were politely attentive. In no time I realized that they were better at the beach game than I, and I was feeling fat in my bathingsuit, and miserable and bored, so I left the shore to them.

And to you, dear reader, I leave it as well. But if among your friends there shall be found one such as I (it's said they crop up once every other generation) who, bravely withstanding its scenic value, abhors going to the beach, let me give him/her my word of homely wisdom:

Go native. Put your roots down in Cape soil and let the city be your place of frivolity. That way you never have time to get to the beach in summer, and can spend the winter beside the hearth with a good book. And you can hell it up in town when the spirit moves. Welcome to the club!

Summer Rental

They say you can rent anything on Cape Cod during the season, even an old cranberry shed. A city friend called recently wondering whether he could rent the old house, long deserted, at the end of our road.

We didn't see why not, but, "Have you been in it?" we asked.

"I've driven by," he said. "It looks very nice. Just what I want."

"You should go through it first," we said, but he had already hung up.

It does look inviting as you drive by. A fairly recent paint job, white with dark red shutters, gives a fresh look to the well-proportioned two-story framing of about a hundred years ago. Wild roses bloom hysterically on the trellis by the kitchen door, almost obliterating it. Stately, neglected trees line the drive. Nature has taken over unchecked on the fringes of the weedy lawn, however. On one side of the drive a mock orange bush has engaged in a death struggle with a small cedar tree, and on the other, poison ivy encroaches more each year, growing as high as a hedge, and turning the most seductive shades of red and yellow in autumn.

He should have gone inside. He shouldn't take such things on faith. A house is so much more than a shell. We would have told him that we wanted him to check on the various appointments in the rooms, and take note of the rather cheap plumbing and rusted sink. More than that, though, we would want him to get the feel of the place, and make sure that he could get along with it.

Many generations have loosened the boards and balustrade, and the rooms, like the pores of a sponge, have absorbed the personalities of those who lived there. Cobwebs of the past cling to the corners and furniture, and can't be swept away. The air, never fresh, is super-saturated with thoughts and scenes remembered. In fact, the house is inescapably haunted.

Being haunted isn't a bad thing in itself, but you must be in tune with the shades about you or they will drive you out. You will never drive them out. Old shades and young play about in the hall, and creak on the curving staircase. The soft pad of sneakered and bare feet, and occasionally the click of a neat high-buttoned shoe, and the swish of a dust ruffle make a background music as insistent as the surf beside a beach cottage.

What were they like, when the house was new? There are clues—the marble-topped commode, the broken chandelier, the misty ethereal paintings of the Hudson River School—clues everywhere, partly erased by the litter of later years and the intrusion of "modern" improvements.

There are two attics, one with the usual old trunks and broken furniture, the other, swept bare, houses a swarm of bees every spring above one of the windows. Wall-to-wall carpeting downstairs and up seems to have receded from the edges of the walls. Gilded motifs in the wallpaper downstairs suggest a grandeur that could never have been realized in South Orleans almost a century ago.

Books are revealing. Among the usual inconsequential novels and mysteries we found, "Decorum: A Treatise On Etiquette And Dress Of The Best American Society," bought (by subscription only) by Susan M. Mayo in 1876, encased in a brown and gold cover, with the sweet, pale likeness of a fragile young lady of fashion framed like a cameo on the front. "Decorum" is a far more fertile treatment of the subject than that of Emily Post or her followers.

Clues are everywhere, and all around are the ghosts. They greet you at the door and follow you through the halls, upstairs and down. They look out of the windows with you, lie on the beds, eat at the table, swing the old hammock gently out on the porch, and talk incessantly in low tones. They feel with you and think with you.

He has rented it, sight unseen, and insight unseen. We're not responsible for what may happen. We told him he should have looked it over first.

Note Found by the Summer Tenant

Welcome, dear tenant, how are you? Well and strong (I hope!)? Strong and cheerful and optimistic and glad to be in out of the traffic (I'll wager)? Cheerful and friendly and kind to others, even those who used this campsite before you (we pray fervently)?

We tried to turn our hand to making the old dump habitable, but a few words of explanation may be in order...

We never could get the skunk smell out of the north patio. Lysol spray covered some of the pungency and flavor but added flavor of its own. You may have noticed the fetid sweet and sour atmosphere as you came in the front door. What I try to do is to inhale as I get out of the car in the garage and then exhale all the carbon monoxide as I race through the patio. You'll get onto it after a while.

As you came in, a hard wooden bench must have caught your eye. It used to have cushions, but they wore out. I keep meaning to replace them. I picture long winter evenings sitting at the sewing machine in front of the open fire, running them up. I did get so far as to buy the material. It's in the bureau downstairs, the one with masking tape across the drawer with "storage" written on it with a magic marker. (I also left a couple of drawers empty for you. I hope it's enough. You know how it is.)

Feel free to use any of the games you find around. One of the Bicycle packs has a couple of cards missing, the eight of diamonds and the jack of clubs as I remember, and you'll have to buy ping-pong balls—dog got the last of ours. Which reminds me about the cats. Our son has the dogs but we've taken the cats down to the cottage with us. They're sure to find their way back here from time to time. (Whenever you use the wall can opener in the kitchen the sound brings them running from a mile away.) They lean against the door and unless you hiss like a nestful of adders when you open it they flock in and immobilize you rubbing against your legs. Don't feel you should feed them, in fact it's better not to, but they will expect it.

We have tried to flush out all pockets of resistance in the house, but the dishwasher still looks streaky and I can't get the shoe polish off the side of the bathtub. The noise that sounds like a New York City demolition crew at work is just the pump turning on. You get used to it. I can't get to sleep when it's quiet any more. Try telling yourself, thank God it does turn on; you need the water.

The clothes washer works well enough but there is so much rust in the water that you might as well not bother. This explains the color of the sheets. If you use the dryer be sure the dial is on the "Permanent Press" cycle. There's something wrong with the heating mechanism, and otherwise all you get is cold air.

Anyway, we're proud of the clean yellow rug. You should have seen it before—sooty, grimy, covered with cat hairs. Know what we did? We took it right out to the driveway and washed it on the blacktop, rinsing it out with hose. It was a great drying day, so it was barely damp by evening when we took it in, but it rained that night and we haven't seen the sun since. I dare say it will be kind of damp for most of the summer. You get to expect that on the Cape. Then comes mildew, not to mention mold. A good strong bleach solution works pretty well on either, and there may be some of that Lysol spray left.

We moved down to the cottage a couple of days ago, and of course I found there were quite a few things needed there, so that's what happened to the vacuum cleaner, in case you're looking for one. Then—I hope you don't mind—I took the ironing board because it's the one I'm used to and you can't buy that kind anymore. I also needed the pencil sharpener but I didn't want to unscrew it, so I spent last evening sharpening a summer's worth of pencils. That's why there aren't any around the house.

I hope you will water the flowers. If, you don't they'll die. We emptied the trash barrels a few days ago, but I notice quite a bit has accumulated since. If you go to the dump on Sundays you'll run into everyone you ever knew.

When the telephone rings twice, it's for us. Just take the message or send somebody down for us, because the cottage doesn't have a phone. We'll be thinking of you up there often, sleeping in our beds and using our things. Have a glorious summer!

Solicitously,

—*Your landlord*

Private Eye

We live high on a hill, at about the eye level of a bird in flight, and many of them take a gander at us in our glass house as they fly by. This gives them something to do and we like to feel they enjoy it as they bank out over the bay, clucking at the goings on.

But they needn't be so smug, because two can play at that game and we get a good look at them too! And we see far more than the naked eye can take in, for our prying eye is clothed in a potent telescope with a 30 power lens, which stands on a tripod in our living room.

We not only see birds with this telescope through our vistavision windows, but we see Everything That Goes On In the Bay—Everything—in Detail. In far less than six miles square we see enough to give us material for a shelf full of best sellers, from the Bobbsey Twins type to the Peyton Place variety.

For we look out on the Narrows through which nearly all boats pass on their way from Big to Little Bay and back again, and many of them stop at the island on the way through, or along the shore here or there. It has been a lively summer. When we learn to read lips a new dimension will be added.

Who wants TV when life's panorama unfolds before them, magnified to hair-raising clarity and detail, with no commercial to stomach acidly? Who wants to cook, sew, clean, iron or go to work, when true life's soap opera is being serialized endlessly through this cinematelescope of human nature?

But it isn't all gaiety and gossip. There was the cold October day when we saw the scallop fisherman's overloaded boat begin to swamp in the choppy Narrows, and the night we noticed that the flashing buoy wasn't flashing; the freighter we spotted foundering off the outer beach with its engine apparently out of commission. There is responsibility here that we never had before. Perhaps we should restrict ourself to watching birds.

And it has occurred to us fleetingly that it has been sort of unsporting of us to be able to spy on our island neighbors as they go about their daily chores, blissfully unaware, but we have not let the thought break our spirit. It's a good thing we haven't, too, for our son came home the other night and said,

"Hey Mum, you know those people over on the island?"

"Ay-yuh—?"

"Well, they've got a telescope just like ours!" And we live in a glass house...Ay-yuh is right!

Truro

The spray along the foam-fringed shore of Truro
shines in the sun as far as eye can reach;
and dark, a masterpiece of chiaroscuro
the cliffs throw shadows far across the beach.
The love of God and glacier, wind and sea—
the lines and furrows of unhurried age
molded the hills and valleys tenderly
and with unerring patterns set the stage.
The actors:—pastoral, the grazing sheep—
or wild, the deer and geese; salt-crusted men
whose long sea-struggles dramatize the deep
eternal theme of death and life again.
The slow resurgent climax never palls;
the encores never end. No curtain falls.

My Favorite Cape Cod Summer

I couldn't have predicted it, but looking back now, if I had to crown one best summer out of 50 on the Cape it would have to be my first, in 1937. I was in love, and the object of my desire had close family connections overlooking Pleasant Bay at the Narrows, to assure our welcome. The close family connections turned out to be an extended family of 30 or more, at least 20 of whom would be at Pleasant Bay Narrows at a time, living in the main house (slept 15), the house next door (Uncle Charlie and Aunt Helen's, slept six or seven), or the upstairs garage, which in those days was a dorm for four or five boys, no plumbing.

My own was an unextended family. I had to get used to the other kind, but it has sustained me ever since.

My previous youthful summer experiences had been at our winter home in what was known as Boston and vicinity, except for a few early experimental summers my parents tried out in Cohasset, where we learned to swim and sail and play tennis like other folk, to prepare us for invitations to friends' summer places, since they were to be our only hope for escape later on.

Escape to Maine, for instance, or, when you come right down to it, to the Cape.

By summer, 1937, I had been to Maine more than a couple of times, and gave the state very high marks, especially the Mt. Desert area where the mountains swept down to the sea, and the air was dry and cool (but the water downright cold, and the beaches rocky). I even learned to canoe at a camp in the Belgrade Lakes region, where I worked for a couple of summers in the early '30s. Not bad, I thought.

So I felt the Cape had a lot to live up to when I first went down. But my male companion promised tennis and sailing and good beaches, so it was worth a try. We were both going to college summer school that year in the Hub area, and weekends cried out to us for what the Cape had to offer. And when the six-week summer school was over there were still a few hot weeks to find relief from before Labor Day clamped down on our frivolities.

71

I learned a lot more that summer on the Cape than I did in summer school. It took a while to sink in, because what I was in (except for the swimming) was culture shock. I felt the way Alice must have felt in Wonderland, after the rabbit hole: startled, curious, intrigued and slightly apprehensive—but hopeful.

The Narrows were, and still are, at the end of a very narrow, windy, bumpy one-track dirt road almost a mile long, which in effect isolated the family members from the world we all knew outside, so they were free to develop their own culture. The way they lived there was different; so were their customs, and for a while I thought they must be talking a different language, because I didn't get it, whatever they were saying, that first summer.

But that didn't mean things were out of control. It was a fiefdom there, and the head honcho was Mon's grandfather, Dr. William Davis, Gampa to family members. His three daughters were powers behind the throne. Among them, Mon's mother (later my mother-in-law and known as Granny) was to be Gampa's successor. She was a very athletic, talented woman who helped run the show, and played tennis into her '90s. She made soap out of kitchen drippings, and in early September filled shelves with beachplum and wild grape jelly. She taught me all about the jelly, and I'm still at it today, but I gave up rapidly on the soap when I found out how dangerous lye can be, and when, on asking her if I could add some oil of sandalwood, she reminded me that, "Sweetest she who smells of naught!"

She also often made her own bread until she found out how delicious Millie Goodspeed's was, and Clarence Knowles's. While Gampa carved the roast or dished out Mr. Scott's famous chowder for Sunday dinner, she sliced the bread, and scaled each slice to the appointed recipient off the back of the knife, sometimes way down the dining room table that seated 23. She was allowed to do that but no one else was even allowed to try, for good reasons.

Granny was also a great entertainer. She had an inexhaustible supply of stories, songs and witty verse, and at the drop of a hat she could deliver a flawless rendition of "Casey At The Bat" in the style of DeWolfe Hopper. There was no lack of dropping hats at the Narrows.

Her other two sisters, Aunts Helen and Mamie, were equally powerful in their own spheres. Aunt Helen was an intellectual and also a wonderful cook, and Mamie, who arrived from Minnesota each summer with Gampa and a menagerie of animals, was a planner, family historian, prime conversationalist and a key bridge player.

These were the setters of standards and the makers of rules. Under them was the vast unpredictable swarm of cousins in bathing suits and shorts (except at Sunday lunch when the boys wore sailor suits and the girls India print dresses). The sailor suits were white middies and pants that filled the bureaus of the 'upstairs garage' and nobody remembers where they came from, but no one was embarrassed to put them on, creating a chorus-line-escaped-from-Pinafore look. How come India print dresses for the girls? Another mystery. I found one hanging on a hook in the corner-of-the-room closet when I got there, and dutifully wore it when I'd had my orders so to do.

Some of the rules: Small children may be excused before dessert (meals were LONG in that family.) Boys have to wear a shirt at dinner. Wash your bare feet in the footpail after coming up from the beach. Take a dip before breakfast (for cleanliness sake.) No one was allowed to sail before they passed the swimming test, which was to swim across the Narrows to Sipson's Island and back.

Electricity hadn't found its way over that formidable dirt driveway, so this meant kerosene lamps at night. After hurricanes in later years I was glad to have learned about kerosene lamps. There was a windmill and pumphouse between the main house and garage which brought water to an attic tank, but in windless periods there were no baths taken. The family had a dock out into the Narrows, to dive off, and for coming in and going out by boat, and yes, they had to get a permit for it even back then.

We did get to sail, both day and night, in the family's Baybird, which I was happy to find was enough like the Cape Cod Baby Knockabout I had sailed in Cohasset to make me feel comfortable.

It was at dinner that I had the most difficulty with the language. There was plenty of talk, and at that time I was more interested in what the boys had to say than the old folks. One of them would hurl out a disconnected remark, e.g.: "And they're all blue, Mister!" followed by hoots of laughter. Then: "I'm calling the hand in your hat!" More hysteria. Mon explained to me later that they were quoting from movies they'd seen (several times) and memorized. I didn't buy it. I knew they were all Mad Hatters.

I look back on that crazy summer with a lot of affection. It was before World War II when we lost a brother and brother-in law, before Vietnam when we lost a favorite nephew. Their names are memorialized in stones in the seawall facing the Narrows.

I remember sailing with Mon out past the house at night, seeing the flickering lights of kerosene lanterns through the window, where the old folks were playing bridge (far into the small hours). We made a pact there and then that we'd never let ourselves get good enough at bridge to be pressed into making a foursome, when what we wanted was to be out there on the Bay. And we never did.

A Cape Codder's September Song

Like gray hairs appearing before the prime of life, poison ivy starts to change color in August, giving us the first hint of verdure's colorful exit. And with September the poke weed's toxic berries purple succulently; the wild dock, edible in spring and ornamental in summer, rusts; the vegetable garden, once so neat with rows of burgeoning largesse, grows voluptuous and disheveled.

Sensing what's ahead, the throat lumps, the brow puckers, the eyes water, the corners of the mouth droop, and the shattered visage takes on that death-is-just-around-the-corner look. But let's not over-react.

September, for all our tears and nostalgia, has as many goodies in its hamper as August or July. To mention just a few, it has Harvest (admittedly a mixed blessing), and it has Freedom from tourists (relatively speaking). It has clear, crisp autumn days, in between the foggy, wet ones, and the hurricanes. It has kids going back to school, and if you didn't get around to buying new clothes for them, it won't matter much after the first couple of days.

September has daddy going back to work, and perhaps better still, mummy, too. Daddy can get along with the same old gray flannels and sports jacket. (Who measures lapels anymore?) As for mummy's wardrobe—September is not for worrying about clothes.

A Cape Codder's till is usually fuller in September than any other month. If he ever gets a vacation he plans it and may even take it now. Labor Day has special significance, as labor eases.

A Cape Codder's September is a jewel in a busy setting. The best days of the year are now, still warm but free of greenhead flies and debilitating humidity. They bring their responsibilities.

Like beach plums, for instance.

Beach plums! Not again!

Again.

But we went through that last year and the year before. Big crops of beach plums *never* come year after year after year.

Says you. Take a look around.

But this is ridiculous. We must have several dozen glasses of jelly in the shed left over. And sugar costs as much as lobster did a few years back.

If you can walk right by those bushes and not lay a hand on them, more power to you. I can't. And then come the wild grapes. And this year you ought to see the wild cherries and apples. It's terrifying. There go three of the best weeks in the year.

Shelves full of empty calories, that's what it brings you. It's just occupational therapy to help you get over the departure of summer friends and frenzies. The beach plum picking addict (or beach plush) doesn't need excuses of course. She needs blinders all summer long so she doesn't know what's coming, and a pre-paid ticket to Arizona come late August.

The vegetable garden buffs are gathering in their harvest too, and there's no predicting it each year. There always seem to be the failures and a runaway success or two. After a few tussles with the latter, I'd settle for the former. Remember our summer of stuffed zucchini boats, each one as long as your arm, which was followed by a zucchini-bread fall, kept going in the freezer? Then came the year when everyone in the neighborhood enjoyed a bonanza tomato crop. They all paid calls on each other, sometimes for the first time in years, to unload their surplus. Tomatoes as big as melons they were, some of them.

There was the autumnal plethora of only slightly buggy turnips we grew last year that were put down in the root cellar in sand, to rot quietly away through the winter.

This year our edible pod peas started blooming and podding in late June and are still at it. The first planting was still doing it when the second planting caught up and kept at it until the third—but no, I guess we never came up with a third! As the quantity increased the quality declined until we were getting pellet-filled inedible stringy and rubbery pods, as limp as a popped balloon.

Give me a few good failures—say Kohlrabi and New Zealand spinach—any day.

But harvesting isn't the only duty on September's roster. Taxes become payable, to be pushed aside as long as possible. Organization responsibilities are reshouldered by special interest groups

and do-gooders. Fund drives are launched. Adult education cours-
es commence.

And the autumn weather turns the leaves to flame, and we
haven't got time for the waiting game . . .

By mid-September tides and sands have erased the scars left
by beach parties; Thanksgiving and Christmas are way beyond the
next horizon; the bogs turn tawny in the sun, camouflaging their
ruby treasures, so never forget that for all the ants that may creep
into a September picnic hamper, it's the best possible month on
Cape Cod. Hallelujah!

And that's confidential.

Goodbye

When the Summer's lobsters are eaten,
And the racing pennants are won,
And the tournament hopefuls are beaten,
And the beach lies bare in the sun,
We shall rest, and faith we shall need it...
(Apologies to Kipling)

Goodbye, all you lovely summer people—goodbye. Goodbye Uncle Bob and Aunt Mabel and Jimmy, Petey, Sandy, Chloe, Susie, Freddy, Ronny and Chuck. Goodbye Cousins Emily and Sam, and Reggy, Janie, Weezie, Piggy and Pat. So long, good fellow elbow-benders at the club, champs at the tee, rivals on the courts, beachcombers, sunbathers, clambakers, swimmers, surfers, anglers, water-skiers, outboarders, inboarders, Beetlecat racers, Baybird, Sailfish, Day Sailer, Whistler, Mercury, Handicap and Chowder racers—So long! Adios, young man with beard, guitar and sandals. Auf wiedersehen, damsel with Godiva hair and bikini. Farewell to you ardent penniless thespians and artists, and you nature lovers and readers of thrillers on porch hammocks. Toodle-oo, beach buggy drivers, surf casters and flounderers, collectors of shells or antiques, campers, counselors, National Seashore visitors, launch lounge lizards and cocktails circuiters.

Pip-pip to young builders of sand castles complete with moat, to diggers to China, and beach construction engineers. Au revior to lollers under beach umbrellas, and barefoot supermarket basket pushers.

Goodbye to the vanishing adolescents, blonde and bronzed, who waited on table at the clam bar, or cleaned cabins, or guarded life at the public beach, or baby-sat, or taught swimming and sailing, and who went to the drive-ins in sports cars and sang "Michael Row the Boat Ashore" at beach parties. God-speed to summer substitute preachers and tutoring college boys.

Goodbye to established writers who mingled generously with admirers at buffets. Hasta la vista to gallery hounds, to musicians playing at casinos and benefits, to riding school pupils and listeners at town band concerts. Cheerio to friends from Dorchester who dropped by on their way to the New York World's Fair. Ta-ta to the school bound, the college bound, the Peace Corps bound, the office bound.

We're so glad you came. It was great! We loved having you. We want you again next summer—in fact we count on it. Summer wouldn't be the same without you. Good luck—work hard—have a successful winter—we'll be thinking of you. It's too bad you can't stay longer, but all good things must come to an end, even the life of the party, and now is the time when we must say goodbye. Good-bye!...(Tom, help the Browns with their bags)...Goodbye!...(Helen, come out and see them off)...Goodbye!...Goodbye.

Oh Youth! Oh Cape Cod! Oh Summer!

Oh to be young on Cape Cod in the summer! Oh to ride unshod over Route 6, 6A and 28 in an open white sports car—white with a wide streak of gold running off-center from bumper to bumper...to ride with honey-streaked hair flying, clad only in a Marimekko shift over a bikini (Oh to be young enough to be able to name the label!)...a bikini the brevity of which serves to accent the unblemished perfection of skin the color of saddle-soaped cowhide...to ride in an open sports car in dark glasses as round as saucers and lipstick as pale as ice cream, beside a young man stripped to the waist with a hairy head and skin the color of integration, or stained teak...to ride beside a young man in shorts that were made by cutting off chinos at the knee and fraying the raw edges, wearing the kind of sandals that have a special thong going around the big toe, who picked up the sports car when he was in Europe last summer...a young man with an auto-harp in the back seat and a couple of University Press paperbacks in the shelf under the dash...

Oh to ride in a white and gold sports car along the Mid-Cape, secure in one's youthful image, stopping for a late lobster lunch and exhibition of Op Art...to wander through Provincetown with the hairy young man in shorts and sandals, needing a native guide and a chaperone, not looking for either, stopping at coffee houses that have an elusive illicitness about their airless underground interiors...to mingle briefly with a summer theatre crowd during intermissions, spotting two or three friends from Connecticut who are down again this summer...to drive off to the beach to take in a couple of the parties, discussing why the last ones were raided and wondering why this one hasn't been yet...

To drive off again wondering where to go next, happy to be too old to observe the driving curfew and too young to want to go home....Oh Youth! Oh Cape Cod ! Oh Summer!

Oh Youth... Oh Summer... Oh Cape Cod !!

Nattering with Norma the Clam

Nattering with Norma the Clam

Norma the Clam

Great Caesar's Ghost

Dear Boss:

I really enjoyed my stretch in the golden west this summer, tasting that fifth great freedom, freedom from responsibility, while you exhumed some of my columnar cadavers. I yearn for more of this fancy-free bon-vivantery, and less of these nagging deadlines. We could have kept it up for a while, warming over the old stiffs, but it had a limited future. In the long run the game gets gamey.

So I'm in the market for a good ghost writer, as the next best ploy. It's the suave, done thing nowadays—I know you'll go along. From prize-fighters to J.F.K they all have words put in their mouths. It's accepted. It's hip.

Don Marquis was the lucky one, finding his copy all typed out for him, single column, by archie the cockroach. As I recall, you used the dodge yourself, boss, when you were living it up editorially with Horace, the seagull who communed with you at the dump. By the way, what's happened to the old fellow? Is the Disposal Area too highbrow for him now? You should keep track of native talent like his.

This was all well and good for you and Don M., but so far I haven't mastered the lingo of the menagerie around me, and none of its literati has mastered this demon machine. To get my kids or a stray friend to bat out the weekly column would mean splitting the pay-check. Does U.S. currency come that small?

What I decided to do was to get a real ghost writer—a ghost ghost writer. It shouldn't be too hard to find one, I figured. When you came right down to it, population may explode like an old-fashioned 4th of July, but there are still more people dead than alive. (And plenty of us more dead than alive, but that's another story). So ghosts should be a dime a dozen, inflation notwithstanding.

And now that extra-sensory perception is really coming into its own, getting in touch with one struck me as child's play. Actually it isn't all that easy, but having fancied the occult since childhood, I thought it would be right in my line. You know that radio feature extra they sandwiched in between discs and commercials that is ushered in by "LISTEN! Listen! Listen listen listen listen?" I was listen-listen-listening a while ago, with the slavish obedience of a captive audience, and was told that extra-sensory perception (ESP) was the topic of the week. A cultured voice then recounted his marked success with this medium of communication. Well, I thought, I'm no medium, but if he can do it I can.

I wanted to pick a ghost that would please us both, boss—one that would understand me and put up with you, if you get what I mean. Salary should be no consideration. A ghost may be presumed to have reached its final reward. You can make out the check to me as usual, with, say, a bonus gesture of appreciation for the double trouble I will have gone to.

I wondered how to choose just the right shade, with so many colorful spirits at large. Should I try Shakespeare? A. Conan Doyle? Emily Bronte? If they weren't already talked out, would they be willing to share my idiom? You would gladly settle for their idiom, no doubt, but we mustn't be accused of cribbing—no more than usual, anyhow. The norm must be preserved.

Yet I shuddered at the thought of tangling with some illiterate phantom who wouldn't know the ropes or get the picture—some glory-hound who might expect a special byline for a series of Ughs. As it turned out, I didn't have much choice one way or the other.

Being a novice, up to now my ESP has only reached what are, perhaps, the lower forms of afterlife. A greenfly, for instance, drank deep of the heady liquor under my left eyebrow the other day, and passed out with intoxication. I dispatched whatever doubt might have remained of him with a brisk swat, and later found myself in ectoplasmic argument with him over whether the swat had been just, under the circumstances. I had, he pointed out posthumously, received only local irritation, whereas I in return propelled him into the nether-nether land before his time. He was in no mood to talk about collaborating over the column, so I let it go, and reactivated my ESP into other channels.

This is done by lying on the beach getting solarized, while easing up on the cerebration. What thoughts flit across my brain are frizzled to the root by the sun's rays, leaving a vacuum that yearns to be filled by messages from beyond.

It wasn't long before my right ear was irrigated by a squirt that seemed to come from what the casual eye might take to be an ordinary soft-shell clam hole. The casual eye would have been deceived. This was a ghostly geyser, a tactful awakening emanating from a clam whose years, dead and alive, it would be unkind to divulge (especially as it turned out to be a she), but to give you a rough idea, let me say that whatever number occurs to you you should add zeros. She spat off a sort of spectral shorthand that I found a lot easier to get down than most of the loquacity you editors expect your reporters to assimilate.

Buried in the sands of eternity, the tides of time wash over her, funneling in the pith of their wisdom as they pass. Scoff if you dare—I'll pit her insight against your seagull's any day—without meaning to be subversive, boss.

In my predicament she was an answer to prayer—a natural! A supernatural! I asked her name, to start things off. Her retort emerged ectoplasmically as, "What's in a name?"

"Oh," I said, "you know Shakespeare?"

"Ask, rather, whether Shakespeare knew me!"

Apparently he did, and this was no time to ask whether professionally, or in a chowder.

"As my ghost writer, I must call you something," I pointed out, "for convenience. How would you feel about 'Norma'?"

"Cool," she said, as closely as I could translate. "Why Norma?"

"I like Norma. Norma is short for Normal, which describes a nebulous condition that no longer exists—like you. And it's long for Norm, which is what we have to preserve in our weekly drudgery."

It's even shorter for Abnormality," she pointed out. "That makes it fine. A name like Abnormality will give me status among my friends. Sure, make it Norma if you like. It's just a matter of . . ." but her words were swallowed up by the incoming tide. I picked up my towel and sunglasses, cheered with the thought that while the moon orbits and the tides flow you and I may have a new copy writer, as long as she doesn't clam up.

Séance-erely yours,

B.C.

Another Spring

"Spring is here, Norma. I don't ordinarily go around telling people about it. I figure they have a right to their own opinion, but I wasn't so sure you were atuned to the seasonal changes, and I want you to know that I stand ready to fill you in."

"Oh, it's Spring, is it? I'm not too aware of time in its flight, but it's better to be filled in than dug out, so go ahead."

"Well, I don't know that I can really do it justice, but I can cite circumstantial evidence. It's not only Spring calendarwise, but when I ventured out the other day I saw crocuses trying to push their dear little heads through the debris. The cat had kittens. The mud thickened on the driveway, making it impassable. The goats began jumping the fence in search of new green pastures. Town meeting's over, and conversation is turning to income tax. All sure signs."

"Oh dear, this means the holiday's finished for me. The party's over."

"Why?"

"Perfectly obvious. During the winter months I don't have much haunting to do, really. The clam bed I've always called my own is relatively free from marauders. I can go where I will—do some sight-seeing, cruise around, have a bit of a vacation. But come Spring, you people start getting itchy with the old clam rake, and I must be back at my post, warding you off."

"Do you ever really succeed in warding anyone off, Norma?"

"Well of course I have to use a spiritual sort of attack. I try to deflect the tines of the rake by working on the soul of the man behind them, turning his attention from fleshly needs. I urge him to relax, enjoying the healing warmth of the sun, pondering deeper values than his appetite. Pretty soon he is stretched out flat behind a dune, deep in the arms of Morpheus. Sometimes he's pretty well blistered by the time he wakes up."

"You and Morpheus are in this deal together?"

"Morpheus isn't really necessary to the operation, though he is handy to have around. I can take care of the job myself. The problem isn't so much to put off the enemy as to distract him."

"Is this all Spring means to you, Norma?"

"That's about the sum of it. Oh, when I was a live clam I used to note a temperature change in the sand and sea—the accompanying sensation of softening of the flesh and feeling of helplessness. We had reactions to the seasons as you do—the cyclical routine, the feelings of anticipation mingled with doubt, the sense of rejuvenation tinged with dread, the mounting hope tempered by bitter experience."

"You sound like a real clam-of-the world, Norma. Didn't you ever, as a young clam, just let yourself go with the sheer joy of living when the Spring sun first penetrated your burrow? Didn't you ever have a mad desire to surface and let the warmth revitalize you?"

"Sure, I tried it once. Know what happened? I was dug up and left baking on the beach. Dehydration set in. Just before it was too late the tide came in, and I dug in in a hurry. The minute you start flitting about on the surface of things you begin to dry up. Isn't it better to be all wet?"

"And so you never smelt the flowers or listened to the songs of birds. I'm terribly sorry for you, Norma."

"Don't be. I've always been able to get spiritual uplift without all those extra frills. Birds and flowers? Transient, fleeting insubstantial whims of nature. Give me a beach, a wide flat beach, nourished by the vigor of the running tide, cleansed by the eternal ocean currents. This gives you the real feel of living—not all that twitter-twatter you talk about."

"Well anyway, Norma, it's Spring, and I like it."

Norma Tries To Get The Picture

Things had been so busy lately that I had left Norma asleep in the deep. I just hadn't been getting to the beach the way I like to. Autumn is the time for the beach. In the autumn you can see the beach and see the sea in uninterrupted splendor. There are no mountains of flesh obstructing the view. With the first cool days the landscape pulls itself together sharply and looks alive.

It's easier to find Norma, now that no one has been trampling around the clam-bed she haunts. Extending my welcoming arms of ESP I make straight for the area north-northwest of the old dory and in no time at all her fountain of ectoplasmic emanation irrigates my senses.

"I'm sorry I haven't been around lately to chew the fat," I said to her the other day, when I finally found time to take a hitch down to the shore.

"Your loss is my gain," she retorted. "Anyway, to me it was only a second ago that we were arguing about fear and security and I told you we're all just a bunch of . . ."

"All right, all right, enough of that. Let's talk about something else."

"O.K., what?"

"You name it. It's your turn."

"I'm not in a very gay mood, I warn you. It's flounder season again. Some of your species have had their hooks hovering around in the Narrows every day and must have hauled in dozens."

"Wonderful! I'd like to take out the rowboat myself and try my luck. I love flounder."

What you mean is you love to eat flounder. There's an important difference. What do you use for bait?"

"Oh, I usually dig a few cl---, seaworms."

"Uh-huh. I know. You hunt around vaguely for seaworms and then dig up a mess of innocent young clams, my descendants, in the prime of life. You people are shameless."

"Norma, at your age your should learn to accept the balance of nature. These things shouldn't bother you any more. You mustn't take it personally. Animals eat plants in the prime of life—we eat animals in ditto—we die and fertilize the soil for plants, and so it goes. It all comes out even in the end."

"I don't see how my descendants are getting much nourishment out of the likes of you!"

"Well, I'm sure it could all be explained scientifically to your satisfaction. Besides, remember, Norma, survival isn't the only thing worth fighting for. You've told me that yourself, and you should know. Let's try another subject."

"As a matter of fact I have something to say about your column. Something worth fighting for as far as I'm concerned. When you use me (and "use" is the word for it) I would appreciate your heading the column with my picture. It's the least you could do. You owe it to me."

"Your picture, Norma? How am I supposed to get your picture? I don't even know what you look like myself."

"Just tell your boss to mosey down here Tuesday night with his Leica. Any time before midnight. It being Halloween, I'll be out and around with all the other ghosts. He may have some difficulty spotting me in the crowd, but I'll come up and introduce myself. You might come along as interpreter, if he's not very spiritually inclined."

"Norma, be reasonable. Tuesday's the busiest day at the paper. If my boss gives any thought to spirits that night it's not likely to be your kind. Anyway, if you're as ethereal as ghosts are supposed to be, a photograph of you would just look like a double exposure."

"Excuses, excuses. I want my picture at the head of your column. I don't care how you go about it, get it there. You can find a way if you really want to."

"I don't really want to. I'm dead against it. By the way, what do you look like?"

I'm a thing of great intangible beauty. Starting with the motif of the clam I once was, a thousand other abstract conceptions, varying with the flow of time and tide, make up my makeup."

"This could never be caught on the prosaic lens of a Leica, Norma. What you need is an artist—an artist of infinite sensitivity and imagination who can embody the abstract in meaning, and meaning in the abstract—who embraces a non-objective permissiveness, yet permits an unobjectionable subjectivity, the subject being you"

"This sounds interesting. Can you come up with one?"

"Well, I know they exist or try to exist (the artist's life is not often a lucrative one), but whether I can funnel one your way Tuesday night is a matter of conjecture."

"It's your duty to start funneling. I'll be waiting, in my best sheet and chain. Don't fail me."

"We might put an ad in the classified section of the Provincetown weekly: 'Ghost Model in search of Artist.' Not that I'm so sure you're a model ghost, but we can give it a try."

"It's up to you. All I care about are the results. Until then, happy Halloween, and boo to you."

"Boo to you, too."

Norma Gets the Picture

Norma gave me an ultimatum a few weeks ago—either I head the column with her picture, or no more copy from her. She is anything but a reasonable woman. I did, however, make her directive known to the public in the October 26 issue, with the following result:

"Dear Madam,

I've taken the liberty of attempting Norma's portrait. I'm afraid there is something wrong with the mouth and I omitted the abstract conseptions (sic), them not being my cup of tea—but isn't the stole becoming?

Yours ever so truly. Helen C. (Mrs. Thomas) Lyman."

This was both thoughtful and industrious of Mrs. Lyman. It warrants a reply:

Dear Mrs. Lyman,

Beyond a doubt, it was both thoughtful and industrious of you to attempt Norma's portrait. From my point of view it is an unqualified success. My judgment may be in question on the matter, since I only perceive Norma in an extra-sensory way, but I have a right to my own opinion, and it is that your artistic materialization of Norma comes through. I feel for it and it reaches me. The mouth is, as a matter of fact, eloquent, and as for the stole, it is more than becoming, it is outrageously flattering. Politically speaking this is a good thing. One must remember that she's not as young as she used to be.

Please do not feel upset about the lack of abstract conseptions (sic). I probably wouldn't know what to do with them anyway. Your drawing has a quality that more than makes up for its want of non-objectivity. Your well-known achievements in the field of medical art have given you the uncanny ability to see through Norma in a precise way that defies the elusive suggestiveness of abstractivity. That you see through her is indicated by the sureness of every stroke of your graphic scalpel. You see through her as we cannot, and tell the truth about her in the graceful manner of the truly great artist, without offending our sensibilities or hurting Norma's feelings too much.

As a matter of fact Norma has given your masterpiece her O.K., though I can't pretend that all her comments were lyrical. She said that she thinks you might somehow have managed to catch her distinguished profile, instead of facing the facts head on, and that her expression would have been more comfortable if she hadn't had so many Halloween responsibilities on her mind. Halloween isn't what it was when she was a ghostling, she said, as she rambled on about the lack of spirit in the younger generation.

"We're having a line cut made of the drawing, Norma." I said, "So we can use it in the paper."

"That's good. I was wondering, though—have you or Mrs. Lyman arranged to have the original portrait put up for auction at the Parke-Bernet Galleries in New York?" she asked. "I understand that Rembrandt's Aristotle Contemplating the Bust of Homer was auctioned there and snapped up by the Metropolitan Museum for $2,300,000. Why wouldn't Norma Contemplating the Ghost of Rembrandt' be a fine companion piece and bring a comparable price?"

"Is the ghost of Rembrandt what they were contemplating, Norma?"

"Well, Mrs. Lyman may title it that way if it seems expedient to her. It isn't the money I'm thinking of, of course. What's money to me, after all! You could probably use it, though, and $2,300,000 does have a resonant ring. But it's the being hung in the Met. Museum that seems suitable to this occasion. I can't think of a more dignified place for a hanging. The National Gallery is too gaudy, and the Boston is too fusty, but the Met suits me and can afford me. I suppose they have good underground vaults at the Met in case of nuclear holocaust, don't they?"

"Norma! I thought you were against bomb shelters! Didn't you say we were all lily-livered?"

"You are, you are—I'm against shelters for anything living. Shelters should only be for things that transcend mortality. People shouldn't be kept, records should be kept—so that some day some super-clam from outer space can drill through the concrete and find, for example, this splendid illustration of soft-shell clamdom rendered by Mrs. Lyman. By the way, when is the official unveiling of the portrait? I want to be sure to be there. It should be quite an affair."

It should indeed. Midnight on the chilly clam flats as the wild geese honk overhead. Of course Norma must be there, and you too, dear Mrs. Lyman! We look forward to seeing you then.

Yours ever so gratefully,

B.C.

Cape Cod Beauties

One day last week the daily paper printed a picture of six smiling beauties meeting at the Red Coach Grill in Hyannis, where they were being "briefed on plans for promoting Cape Cod at the Massachusetts booth at the New York World's Fair." I ran my eye over the toothsome group to see if there was anyone I knew from around here. There wasn't. I wiped my glasses and took a closer look at the caption. No wonder. They were, from left to right: Brockton, Quincy, Lynn, Cambridge, Boston and Lowell. Now as a matter of fact I do know a couple of people from a couple of these towns, but much as I may admire them, they are not among those I would select to promote the Cape, any more than I would pick a garland of fresh blossoms from Nauset Regional High School to promote Brockton, Quincy, Lynn, Cambridge, Boston or Lowell. Especially if they needed briefing, as they would be bound to. Why, I've been briefing myself on the Cape for some twenty years now and know full well that I've only skimmed the headlines. As every native knows, you need the support of five generations of Cape Cod marrow in your bones before you can speak with any true authority on the subject.

Now it is possible that the beauty and allure of these girls will victimize revelers at the Fair to the point where they could be led into the Australian bush or Brazil jungles without a murmur, but Cape Cod doesn't call for this Shanghai approach. The Cape has its own magnetism. It doesn't need the patter of baby dolls from Brockton, Quincy, etc. to heat the blood of the summer invader. And if it's gorgeous dames with a salty flavor that the Massachusetts Booth boosters are looking for why don't they go straight to the source and comb the dunes or glean the bog country for them. They could find as juicy a bucket of beach plums as any tourist could hope to steal away with.

In true Patriot's Day spirit, I took a stroll down to the flats to discuss this matter of Narrow Land pride with Norma, the chatty ghost of soft-shell clam, who is my fellow ESP operator. She picked up my signal directly.

"Look at it this way, Norma," I emanated, "If one of those girls was named Hopkins or Nickerson or Snow, or knew a cranberry scoop from clam rake...."

"Ugh!" she siphoned sharply, "Your imagery is as distasteful as ever, but you're right. It would be far more appropriate to send along a representative indigenous to the locale, one whose roots are buried in Cape Cod sand." She adjusted her spectral stole suggestively (see illustration below).

"If I disinter you correctly then, Norma, you would yourself be willing to take on the assignment?"

"I could be drafted," she admitted coyly.

I hope the Massachusetts booth will take notice and make adjustments.

On the Road Again

On the Road Again

Reuniting the Clan

I said I knew it was outrageous but I had to take three weeks off for a family reunion. "That's one week to get ready, one week to have it, and one to recover," I explained. "Three weeks," said the assistant editor. "Then maybe you should write something about it." And I said, "Sure;" quickly before he could say, "Just kidding."

Family reunions are, after all, about as interesting to the general public as home movies. But to be asked about one is a rarity not to be passed up. So here goes:

The Cape is a wonderful place for a family reunion—the best! But not for us.

We have friends who come down to a big house on Pleasant Bay every summer with their kids and grandchildren and love it. They're away from megalopolis and high pressure jobs or schools. There's plenty to do here, and open space enough so that no one feels trapped.

When I first came to Cape in the late '30s as a significant other to my future husband it was to that very house, and to a group of his relatives who spent whole summers there in perpetual reunion with remarkable success. Their huge combined families included two Uncle Charleys and two cousins named Bill, and I soon felt like a very insignificant other, but looking back on it I can see that it really worked well for all of them, year after year. They had all zeroed in on the Cape from other places to see each other because it's perfect for that sort of thing here.

But not for us.

Not for us, because we live here. Our children were fledged here, and then took flight. When they come back we fall into our old roles; my husband is head honcho, I'm a martyred housewife and our progeny slide back into being sibling rivals. We need new settings to re-establish ourselves with a more up-to-date power base. (Besides, I don't want to do all the cooking.)

A new locale for a reunion is a unifying focus presenting communal challenges. We have tried various spots over the years, starting with Isle Royale National Park in Lake Superior (top drawer, twice repeated), and including Fort Flagler on Puget Sound, Washington (good); a Canadian Provincial Park campsite on Georgian Bay just after it was vacated by a family of black bears (survivable); houseboats on the Trent-Severn Waterway between lakes Ontario and Huron (exciting, piquant); cabins on a lake in central Montana (gorgeous), and an inexpensive but cheerful hotel in the village of Faistenau-bei-Salzburg in Austria where my husband and I worked for a small school during the '80s. That jaunt included a side trip to Venice (awesome).

This time we picked the Isle of Arran, the southernmost of the inner Hebrides off the west coast of Scotland. It had the basic requirements: it was beautiful and largely unexplored by us, inexpensive (very, by Cape Cod standards), not over-touristed, easy to get to (an hour's ferry ride from the mainland) and rural in character. There would be enough to do there, but not too much.

My husband and I had been there several times before as an ideal spot to get over jet lag after a flight to Prestwick or Glasgow, and always thought it would lend itself to a reunion, given passable weather.

We had found a group of "self-catering Finnish chalets" on a hillside beside a stream in the southern corner of the town of Lamlash which took care of the 24 of us with comfort and dispatch.

Arran (not to be confused with the Irish Isle of Aran) is roughly 20 miles north to south, and 10 miles east to west, with mountains in the north, lowlands in the south, a shore road circling it, connecting its garland of small towns and villages, and two narrow inland roads running east and west. It has three castles, two in ruins but one in splendid repair, whose grounds include acres of spectacular gardens. Rhododendrons are a rampant weed on Arran, and many tropical plants survive there because of the temperate climate. There are caves to explore where Robert the Bruce hid from his enemies, standing stones here and there (Helen hugged one of them), burial mounds, sheep farms galore, waterfalls to walk to, mountains to climb, and ponies to trek, though we never did any trekking. You can rent rowboats and sailboats, but we didn't get to them either. That's for Cape Cod. One morning before the main horde of relatives arrived we sat on the grass on castle grounds and watched sheep dog trials which went on all day.

Every town has its small hotels, pubs, restaurants, craft shops, public playgrounds with swing sets, and public toilets (some of them automatic). Roads are narrow and twisty, but buses ride them anyway (on the left, of course). Rental cars are hard to come by, and are only available to those under 70 years old. (Under seventy!! Come on! Two years ago when we were 75 you rented us that clunker with the busted muffler and no rear window mirror;—without a murmur!) Luckily we had progeny with us when we arrived who qualified. We had reserved two smallish cars, but managed to put one of them out of commission after a couple of days, by bringing it in contact with the railing of the narrow bridge over the "bur-r-r-rn" near our cottages.

So how did we all get around? Scheduled buses run around the island every hour or so. Bicycles are an option we tried with success. Hitchhiking is smiled on and expected here. ("Everyone is so nice—they always pick you up.") But how about that old bromide about Scotspersons being dour and stingy? We couldn't find a single one.

Then there are taxis, including taxi vans, which are not expensive, and in our case on a 50-mile round trip included a driver who gave a running account of local history, geology, mythology and gossip, and cheerfully waited an extra hour for our return trip without charging for it.

Yes, we had decent weather and a great time. We had pub and cafe lunches or made sandwiches, went off on small group ventures during the day, with dinners together in one of the chalets each night around eight. Every cottage had a lightweight picnic table with benches, which we combined in Kye's digs, since she didn't seem to mind, and was the accepted Chef Supreme. The five tables took care of all twenty-four of us and even an extra four one night when we were joined by two nieces who live in London and our favorite bed and breakfast hosts from a previous trip.

How can I introduce the cast of characters? It's hopeless to try to do justice to each member of our hefty tribe, so all I can do is throw in names at random and let the chips fall where I hope I can duck out of the way. We were our immediate family—children, grandchildren, spouses (except for Ron, back home looking after the farm in Vermont). And there were four significant others (who aroused my deep affection, admiration and sympathy, and without whom we couldn't have corralled four significant grandchildren.)

What did we do? We climbed Goatfell, more than half of us, on two miraculously clear days. This highest mountain on Arran has always had its head in the clouds when we have been there before. We fished, just a few of us, for hour after hour after hour, with enthusiasm but no catch worth keeping. It's the process that counts. We craft-shopped and wandered around. Teresita took pictures, good ones, but had a light leak in one of her cameras which gave a UFO-effect to a few of the results. We all spent an afternoon walking to the King's Caves, where we left a message under one of the stones near the entrance for Susan McKey of Chatham and Philadelphia who will be there in August. That night we had dinner at the Kinloch Hotel in Blackwaterfoot and listened to an indigenous group of talented musicians play local instruments and sing for us, a special deal that Mon arranged for his aged parents and clan.

One of the rituals that crops up regularly at these gatherings is the production of The Skit. Helen, as chief proponent, orchestrates it and comes up with a game plan. Mon, her brother, wants no part of it. Tom, essential if somewhat reluctant, is the key stand-up comic. Kye wrote a lot of it and performed brilliantly along with Paul, Colin and assorted grandchildren, in this case Duncan, Heather, Halleck and Teresita. We, the target audience, were kept mostly in the dark until the finished product, although we couldn't avoid hearing explosions of self-panicking laughter bursting from chalet rehearsals. Finally I rebelled, and got let into a final rehearsal, and was even given a couple of lines.

It was fun, and very funny, we thought. Would it play in town hall? Who can tell nowadays? But not to worry. The strength and beauty and point of a family reunion is in the reuniting, and this we all did with pleasure.

Three Coins in the Laundromat

One of the things that is wonderful, wonderful about Copenhagen is its laundry facilities. It seems to have at least as many laundromats as Rome has fountains, with as much of the populace putting coins in them. How like the Danes to be so clean and considerate!

It was a month since we had seen the inside of a laundry establishment. Our slivers of Cashmere Bouquet stolen from jet liner washrooms were reduced to translucency, and our wrinkle-free wardrobe showed marks of many curtain rods over which it had been slung to dry. It was time for a good thorough washing. I gathered everything into plastic bags and set out on that crisp morning, light of step.

I was light of heart also. This was home-type activity for me, and much of the daily round in Europe couldn't make that claim. I pictured putting in a quiet hour or two sitting in a fetal position in front of the machine, watching our clothes go round and round.

I found women and machines in assorted sizes looking tidy and businesslike at the laundromat a few doors away. I tossed my stuff into a vacant machine, and started to dig around in my change purse for coins that would fit the slots provided. No such luck. To begin with, one slot was square. Another was the wrong size and had purposeful but ambiguous little red and green lights beside it. In fact the whole instrumental panel was quite different from ours. I looked around for help. There were instructions on the machine and walls, so I studied them carefully. I have always believed that if you concentrate on a foreign language hard enough its basic message will come through, in the mystical sort of way we are all bound to one another. I concentrated.

"1. Fyld maskinen med løst ikke sammendoldet tøj," said the first instruction, "luk døren omhyggeligt. Stil konten på det ønskede program," it went on, "anbring poletten tryk håndtaget 1 bund og maskinen starter met et forskyl." I felt the word "program" proved my theory and "starter" was the clincher. Clearly one was supposed to program the starter—but how?

"Does anyone here speak English?" I asked desperately. Apparently no one did. Most of the busy ladies looked embarrassed for me, but one of them looked up and spoke volubly in her native tongue. I have always believed that if you listen carefully enough to a foreign language spoken, its basic message will come through, in the mystical way we are all bound to one another. I listened very carefully but could not interpret my findings in the time allotted. She decided to demonstrate, as one does to a small child. She selected three coins from my change purse and, lightly grasping me by the arm, led me to a wall-dispenser I had overlooked in the corner. She fed the machine, which spewed back several oddly shaped disks. Then, taking a plastic cup from the top of a washer, she went over to another dispenser for soap. It mattered not that I had brought my own soap. Clearly one was required to buy a measured amount of detergent in a plastic cup by inserting a disk. She did, and then started the machine with the other disks, waited for a green light, inserted half the soap—waited for the green light to go out leaving a red light on and then tossed in the rest of the soap through another input area. I attended with deep admiration until I thought I had it all straight.

For the second load I was on my own again, barring the distracting audience of a son and his friend, who came in to help. With studied nonchalance I strolled over to the coin dispenser and plopped in the designated øre. Then without hesitation I sauntered over to the other dispenser and slapped the soap disk in its slot. Out poured the soap onto the shelf and then onto the floor. I scooped up as much as I could into a plastic cup while all the kind ladies looked politely away. The machine disk turned out to be for a larger machine than the one my clothes were in, but I made the shift and proudly explained the red and green light system of soap insertion to the boys.

"Når pilen når gront felt kan skyllemiddel itlsaettes 1 saeberum," I pointed out. "Når rød lampe slukker er vasken faerdig døren kan åbnes efter ca 20 sekunder."

"I wonder where these machines are made," said my son's friend. "It was a lot easier back in Wyoming where I come from." He went over and looked at the manufacturer's label.

"H. Greenwald Co., Brooklyn, N.Y."

"Oh well," I said, "they keep you on your toes."

When we left I caught the eye of the nice lady who had come to my rescue.

"Thånk yøu ever sø much før åll yøur help," I said.

Summer Cruise

This is the sort of cruise you like to reminisce about," said Marybelle. And as September is a memory month for us, we may as well reminisce.

Picture, if you will, crisp blue days, star studded nights, curved white sails meeting the wind's challenge. Picture our husband aloft, lean and tanned, crosslegged on the crosstrees, shouting "Ahoy!"; at the helm our brother-in-law Will, lean and tanned, scanning the horizon; abaft the beam, manipulating the fishing rod with practiced hand, our sister-in-law Marybelle, and us in our new aqua bathing suit on the forward deck soaking up that final layer of tan that is to last all winter.

Picture all this, because it is just what we pictured when we said, "Sure, we'd love to" to Will's suggestion that we join them for a short cruise to New London in the 32' ketch, "Maid of Orleans."

It didn't actually start raining until we were loading supplies into the skiff before departure. It didn't actually stop until we reached New London, although there were moments of varying intensity in between. There was a torrential downpour at Cuttyhunk at midnight, for example, that filled to overflowing the bowls we had taped over the leaks in the cockpit. There were the hours of intermittent drown and drizzle off Cotuit when we all sat in the cockpit in foul weather gear, ready to give dramamine the lie at the leeward rail at any time. The coast was sliding stealthily by, barely visibly through fog and rain, with dead trees standing stark above the beach grass and dunes.

"Existentialist stage set," we observed in the tone of one who calls M. Sartre "Jean" or "Paul." No reaction from the crew.

We went on and on and on and on and on. The rain drove down endlessly, pock-marking the choppy waves. Everything was bathed in an eerie green-gray light, which we said must be heralding the approach of St. Vitus Dance.

"St. Elmo's Fire," Marybelle said tersely, "is what you mean. That's all we need," she added. She agrees with us on the proper female behavior on 32' ketches. Not for us the swarming up and down the rigging or trimming of the jigger without being told. Such is for rawboned leathery windswept women with faded blue eyes to match their denims and salt matting their hair. For us are long patient hours of suffering sitting quietly, damp, cold, brave.

"Most wives," Marybelle pointed out, "wouldn't be seen dead going on a cruise at all."

"You mean we're Good Sports?" we asked hopefully.

"Sort of," she said, "everything considered."

There were moments of wild excitement. The mizzen ripped. The skiff nearly swamped and had to be hauled aboard by our mighty men, while the ship lurched and yawed, and Marybelle handled the tiller and we tried not to be sick. It was obvious to us that they would all be swept to sea and we would be left to bring the boat in alone. We were reminded, and reminded everyone else, of the recent Atlantic story about the woman whose husband died at sea and had to be brought in to port on ice in the hold with the fish.

Once when we were dismally pitching and tossing about in the open sea out of sight of land we hauled a square red foam rubber cushion aboard that we found bobbing about like a little raft. We could only assume that its ship had gone down with all hands.

To be fair to the Chamber of Commerce, these were the only consecutive days of rain all summer. It began to let up as we approached New London late one evening, hungry.

"Thank God we're almost there," said Marybelle. "This is the sort of cruise you like to reminisce about." she said "afterwards."

How to Beat Traffic

Most of us repress the memory of that hot summer day a few years ago when traffic on the way to Nauset Beach slowed to a final stop—a dead stop, as rigor mortis set in with the sun beating down brutally hour after hour.

At first everyone honked and shouted about. Then they got out, locked their cars and walked the rest of the way, those who could make it. They looked like a horde of refugees, grimly plodding along, sweating freely, dropping off bits of baggage by the side of the road whenever they felt overballasted—surf boards, beach chairs, Frisbees, six-packs, left free for the looting.

Some people said later that the cops should have arrested them for littering and parking so as to obstruct. Others said the town could have charged the regular car beach-parking fee all the way back to the town center, since the road became a vast extension of the beach parking lot. As it was, officials had enough trouble getting people and cars turned around and home again. They weren't up for listening to advice or wise remarks.

That's no way to spend summer on the Cape now, is it? We don't want it to happen again, do we? Be advised, traffic is already slowing to an ominous creep. If we don't act it will soon be too late. Don't think it's the other guy's job to stay off the roads you're taking. It's up to each and every one of us to do his/her part to negotiate a settlement with the traffic problem without resorting to violence and terrorism.

For starters we could try an every other day system. Names starting with A-M get to take to the roads on Mondays, Wednesdays and Fridays only. The N-Zs get T-Th-S, with Sundays free for all. The daily working crowd can bike, jog, hitch or make excuses on their grounded days.

Or we could alternate year-rounders and tourists on the M-W-F, T-Th-S system, or divide along political lines, or just men/women? We could turn Main Street, East Orleans and Nauset Beach Road into pedestrian malls. There could be a massive parking lot out by the dump, with b-Buses to ferry us back and forth.

Maybe some inventive entrepreneur will come up with a flying beach blanket (solar or wind powered, preferably).

Or we can forget the beach and town and spend the summer home on a hunger strike. Starting in mid-July, we should just be able to make it through Labor Day if we're as tough as the Irish.

But enough of this idle daydreaming. My sister, who is also a neighbor and comes over on foot, has a simple non-violent solution she has used for years. "After June 15," she says, "it's right turns only. Plan things so you don't have to go left, because you can't. It's tricky to do this, and you need a map, but it's a matter of survival."

She makes a profound observation here. Trying to turn left is what screws up both lanes of traffic all summer long. From her home on Horseshoe Lane in South Orleans she turns right onto Davis Road, right onto Quanset, right onto Route 28, sweeps right into the South Orleans General Store and Post Office area, does errands there, sweeps out again, turning right. On into Orleans to the second set of lights. Here she goes straight, negotiates a sharp right around the acute angle of the triangle in front of the Wheelhaus Cafe (where Beth Bishop's used to be), right again onto Main Street, and right into the Orleans Post Office parking lot. Then, after tending to various affairs nearby, she can exit back onto Route 28 again and go home, or take a right onto Main Street and head for Snow's, which is more sporting. There is a way for her to get back from Snow's, right turns only, but I hesitate to go into it. If all of our South Orleans readership starts using her route it could make traffic a bit thick for her, and she might stop coming over here on foot anymore.

But I can tell you this: it's no great shakes of a route, but it beats hunger striking at home, fretfully awaiting that great traffic jam in the sky.

Kidcity

If you wonder where they went, those summer kids with guitars and bare feet, the part-time restaurant and supermarket help who spent the night in lofts or six-to-a-rooming houses or on the beach, as their hair grew lighter and longer and skin grew darker as Labor Day approached—if you wonder how far their VWs and sports cars took them, I have good evidence that they got as far as Marlborough Street, Boston, with some spilling over to Commonwealth and Beacon Streets. There they took up residence in six-to-a-rooming houses and apartments and have been collecting parking tickets and folk-rock recordings during the cold winter afternoons sweating out the weekends and their grade point averages.

In the mornings most of them go to school. Boston has long been a city for students to come to because of the colleges in and around it. Lately, though, since the college mania has become big business, new colleges have been coming to Boston because of the students in and around it. In this way the body urban maintains homeostasis regardless of drop-out rates, while becoming more and more adolescent all the time. The Age of the Boston Brahmin and Boston Irish is relegated to the annals of the dusty past, for this is the Age of the Boston Kid. Kids are taking over the city. Though most live on Marlborough Street, their influence is blanketing the Back Bay and Beacon Hill area. The island of adult activity is shrinking nervously into the State and Congress Street compound, and may eventually move out to the suburbs completely.

The new Kidcity enjoys Kidrule. The Boston police have for the most part abdicated. When they come around on their rounds, if round their rounds they come, they just slip parking tickets under windshield wipers, and drive along hastily. The apartment owners live in Newton or Dorchester, or Somerville, or Lynn, and have unlisted telephone numbers. They too have abdicated.

But this is not to say that mayhem reigns. Not at all. Most of the time things go along in fairly orderly fashion. (I made a few sociological jottings during the three weeks I stayed there.) At eight in the morning the streets are alive with kids, apparently going somewhere. Then everything is peaceful on Marlborough Street until about two in the afternoon, when a little pop-rock wafts down through the ceiling or up through the floor, occasionally accompanied by live guitar. Weeknights are uneventful except for the inevitable whine of tires skidding on ice.

Then come the weekends. Friday and Saturday are orgy nights in the Hub. Every apartment has open house and every kid goes to every other kid's party. All night long they are running up and down stairs and in and out of rooms and front doors. All night long the players are caterwauling, pop bottles breaking and kids reeling through the streets. They never seem to be quite drunk or quite sober. Whether they have been smoking pot or getting hopped up with dope my jottings don't tell me, but at around two in the mornings knots of boys gather in the streets and engage in mock battles. There is none of the vicious tension of West Side Story, or the vicious ugly temper of bar room brawling. The kids just yell a few challenging insults at each other and wave their arms around in attitudes of threat. Sometimes they roll a trash can into the street or throw a pop bottle at a window, but not often. Mostly it's just yelling and threatening.

Sunday they sleep it off, and Monday they are back on the streets at 8 am, apparently going somewhere.

In June they will head their sports cars southeast again leaving behind them their weekends and grade point averages, and the rows of parking meters saying Violation.

—●

Crossing Bridges

To the Editor:
Dear Sir:

In tidying up odd bits of unfinished business so that I may give 1965 my undivided attention, I find that there is one thing between us—that is, I owe you a letter concerning the Verrazano Narrows Bridge connecting Brooklyn with Staten Island that you wrote about editorially a while back. What I should have done, of course, was to rush in and stop the presses before you became so embarrassingly entangled. A Cape Codder should never get hung up at such a height so far from his native soil. But it's done, and I can only try to help you down to earth.

As I remember, your point was that while the bridge might be all very well and good as a bridge, all it did was connect one nothing-of-a-place with another nothing-of-a-place. Later on, in your December 17 Letters Column, Jeff Newman deftly questions the validity of your implying the need of a bridge to lead anywhere, suggesting that its purpose for existence could be the great wonder of "being." He is, of course, right, and you should have thought of that. But whether or not we must cherish existence for existence's sake, I set out this past holiday week to test your thesis empirically—does the breathtaking arch in fact connect something worth mentioning with another.

I started from Cape Cod (which you had darn well better think is something worth mentioning) with the intention of connecting my daughter with her job among the fossils at the Smithsonian Institute in the nation's capital (which you had darn well better think is something worth mentioning).

We hugged the coast as closely as we reasonably could and still make time, and this of course meant lashing the wheel along the Connecticut pike and letting the wake of the trucks suck us along, with one of us standing watch, to toss two bits out the window every time we went through a toll gate, like throwing garbage to the seagulls. Well there comes a time when any Cape Codder on the road to Washington, or any V. I. P. coming the other way (and as we all know it's a reversible reaction) has to decide whether to go over the George Washington Bridge or through the tunnel and come face to face with the temptations of New York City, or go way around by the Tappan Zee Bridge in Tarrytown and through Westchester and Newark and all that. Well, the first is out of the question if you really want to keep going, and as for the second, you might as well go by way of Canada and Detroit and avoid Newark too.

Not any more, though. Now there's another choice. Now you can keep the wheel lashed, hugging the coast, leaving the World's Fair Grounds to starboard, and after a series of short tacks, sail up onto the Varrazzano Narrows Bridge, run right across Staten Island planing all the way and not come about until you find yourself heading out of New Jersey, and from then on, back to the pipe berths to sack out until you hit D. C. We tried it and it works.

The fact is, boss, when the fog clears you're going to find the V. N. Bridge connects Cape Cod with the nation's capitol—that's what you're going to find, and does it very prettily too. Now whether this is a good thing or not could feed you editorial material for the next four years or more, but we'll cross that bridge when we come to it.

Archly,

B. C.

Edge Pieces

Cape Codders make longer portages each year. It used to be enough to lug the lapstrake from Bay to Backside and back, but now sailfish and surfboards are carried aloft from Cape Cod to Long Beach, California, and the other way. I recently followed the surfboard trail from coast to coast, both by air and over macadam, and took a few notes, in case you're interested. Me, I didn't take my surfboard along, much as I love surfing, but I tucked a magic carpet in my money-belt just in case. I wasn't going to get stuck in the middle somewhere, a thousand miles from shore!

If you leave with the jet set, as the wind is dying over the Bay in the late afternoon, you can have five hours of radiance and glory and still arrive to see red sails in the sunset—the same sunset, the same day. The old wrinkled skin of the great United States will have unfurled beneath you like a huge mainsail—Alleghenies—Mississippi—Rockies—Grand Canyon—Lake Mead—Death Valley, as you run toward the sun as if it were a channel marker, as indeed it is. Coming back by car, of course, is different. Then you are likely to make racing buoys of various cities and tack along the turnpikes, hailing Salt Lake City, St Louis, Chicago and Cleveland as you go by.

One thing comes clear enough. The Mountains are high and snowy and the lakes are deep and wide; the cities are full of people; horses and cattle roam the ranges, and corn grows heavy in the corn states, but it always feels good when you get to the coast. Even in California the water looks good, and the sight of the beaches makes you start nudging out of your sneakers. You may not find Bay scallops, but the fellow at the filling station can tell you how he fixes abalone steaks in his spare time (you take it out of its shell like a snail, and then you slice it and pound it with flour to make it tender.) You kind of feel at home as you head north on California Rte 1, smelling the flats and watching the kids surf. The porpoises and whales at Marineland have almost as much charm and showmanship as the mermaids off Nauset on a misty night. Some of the stuff you buy in Carmel might just as well have been metalwrought or leathercraft in P'town.

The country's like a jig-saw puzzle. All the important pieces that hold the picture together are the edge pieces. You always want to start with the edge pieces and it's the edge pieces that give the clues of what it's all about. Once you get them in, everything else falls in place.

And when you get home after a long portage you realize that the greatest of all edge pieces is Cape Cod, no matter how screwy and out of line it may look. This is a good thing to know, even worth carrying a balsa raft from sea to sea to find out.

SECTION 6
Word Play

Dear Sir

"D ear Sirs," we write to the electric company, or the local draft board, or the mail order company that didn't refund our money after we returned the cracked china. But they are only dear to us in the expensive sense, and we know they know it, and they know they know, so whom are we kidding with this "dear" stuff? Why, I know plenty of people who don't even call their near and dear "dear" and yet they "Dear Sir" their business letters without a qualm. We are even more hypocritical when it comes to saying goodbye. "Yours truly" we say, or "Sincerely yours," untruly and insincerely. To pretend even for a moment that we are theirs, and compound the reception with emphatic adverbs adds insult to injury.

Of course, since we are only following convention, the sirs (if they are sirs, sometimes they're women, and any day now they may become machines) readily see through the front, and know that if we say we are theirs sincerely we feel cool toward them, and if we say "truly" we feel icy. How then can we show it if we actually do feel rather chummy toward our dear sirs—if somehow we feel that a spark has been kindled between us worthy of acknowledgement? Convention leaves us flat. Nothing has been devised to fill the gap between "sincerely" and "affectionately" that doesn't sound self-conscious, embarrassing or contrived. "Cordially" is flaccid and indecisive. "Respectfully" is too respectful, and "Humbly" too humble. "Ever thine" is la-de-da; "As ever" is ducking out of the problem; "Toujours" is affected; "Your friend" is gauche; "In haste" is redundant; "Sympathetically" or "Gratefully" sounds strained. Probably the most acceptable solution would be to start letters with "Sir:" and end with "goodbye." It does seem, though, as if this might be a chance to put all those adverbs that have been dropped from common usage into service again. While we may start quick, "go casual" and play it cool through life today, we can at least end our letters, "Casually," "Coolly" or "Quickly." We should be able to wind them up sadly, hopefully, wordily, sentimentally, winsomely, patronizingly, anxiously, brilliantly, humorously, acidly, wearily, uneasily, wistfully, cheerfully. With a little imagination and lot of "ly's" we may, if we like, bring about an adverbial renaissance. We can run the gamut from indifferently to intimately, from furiously to gently, from coldly to heatedly. But first it is necessary to get out of the rut.

Within the rut, it is interesting to note that when no favorable adverb seems adequate, we simply say "Love" yet at the opposite extreme, we rarely say "Hate." We don't even use "Hatefully" very often. Perhaps we should. Why shouldn't our letter reflect our un-inhibited emotions, good or bad? Why shouldn't we sound as sick as we are? Maybe the art and vogue of letter-writing will return if we drop the polite packaging and rip right into it, swinging. I'd be much more likely to read a letter that started, "Ignorant, Forgetful Madam," and closed, "Angrily" or "Impatiently" when a magazine wants me to re-subscribe than I am with the usual "Dear...Sincere-ly" routine. And not only would letters regain their rightful position in literature, but the language would become more openly colorful, epithetically speaking.

—●

Cages

Fifty years ago, or so—
(I do remember)
first we built the cages—
fourteen line, five-stress iambic cages—
four-stress couplet quatrain cages
complete with rhyme-scheme shackles,
rules and restraints.

And then we tried to fill them.

It was safer that way.
At least we had the cage to show for it.
"A sonnet !—Well—nice work," you might expect,
even when you hadn't caught the tiger
alive, to fit the cage with fourteen bars.

Dog-tooth Days

R inse," said the dentist, momentarily removing his instrument of torture, nodding toward the flowing bowl beside me. I spat into the spiraling waters.

"What you mean is 'Spit,'" I remarked. He smiled politely. We both knew it was quibble. He knew I knew that he wasn't trying to couch an uncouth term in Victorian euphemism, and I knew he knew I knew.

He probably also recognized that I was grabbing the chance to say something, no matter what, while the tongue was free, accepting the old challenge to see how many words I could get in edgewise between the drill and other bits of dental hardware. He soon had my tongue cornered and cowering again, and the conversation was closed as far as my taking part in it was concerned. A hooked tube sucked away any further inclination to spit or rinse.

Actually I had a point, however trivial. Since there was at the time no Dixie cup from which to sip, all I could have done was spit. To say "rinse" was to overglorify. He could have parried, if he'd wanted to lower himself to an argument, by observing that a squirt of water he had given me had turned the whole process into one rinsing, with spitting only a subordinate part, and I in turn would have countered by pointing out that while he may have provided a rinsing situation, all I could provide, at his urging, was a spitting situation.

Together we rinse, divided I spit, I concluded, giving myself the last word in the fictional exchange. I then abandoned myself to the inevitable, to the muted strains of Strauss waltzes and Peer Gynt punctured by sudden shrieks from the new jet-age drill. Clutching the arms of the chair I urged my mind into billowy recollections of bygone days.

I remembered a dentist I knew in my youth who used to say "Rinsy-winsy," coyly, to his more decorous customers, to take the curse off mention of the indelicate act, and was known to come out with "Spitty-witty," when he wanted to be more specific. But that was before this present gentle jaw-breaker was born.

"What mark does dental care leave on human relationships?" I pondered. I remembered a time when shortly after acquiring my second teeth I spent a vacation at a camp in the Adirondacks with my parents. Other families were enjoying the same privilege. The son of one such was just enough older than I to earn my instant admiration, and an acute ecstasy came over me when I discovered what kind of toothpaste he used, by spying the tube lying on a rock beside the mountain stream. It was Ipana. For years afterwards I let Ipana froth around in my mouth morning and night as a symbol of constancy, although I never made any headway with the boy, and rarely caught even a gleam of his teeth in my direction.

In contrast, there was a house-party I went to as a girl, where, facilities being limited, we had to more or less line up for a chance to wash, etc. Ahead of me one morning was a cleancut youth of heroic grace and deportment, who, though he never had much to say, was indeed a maiden's dream. Through the thin walls the sounds of his toothbrushing were crisply audible. You could picture the whole thing, clearly.

First there was a brisk vibrating sound like a rivet piercing granite. This went on for some time, varying in pitch according to the area under attack. Spitting followed like a series of sharp reports from a popgun. Then a prolonged whooshing sound like the start of a 4th of July rocket as he moved into eliptical polishing. Then a low hollow roar, sounding as I have imagined a faraway moosecall might sound, which proclaimed the thorough cleansing of the tartarous regions in back. Then a long exploratory rinse and a gargle. Another rinse, and again a gargle. Then the firm plink, plunk of dental floss breaking through. Another far reaching rinse. And finally the soft squeak of fingers massaging gums.

The estimable young man will surely carry his antiseptic grin unmarred to his grave, but after that ordeal I could never greet it with better than a bacterial grimace.

My dentist would consider such an attitude blasphemous, sounding, as it does, as if I were against proper home dental care. He might even suggest that he could find sour grapes sticking in my teeth. A riveting in time, he might add, saves nine.

When he finally uncouched my tongue from its bed of cotton bolsters, he scraped around a bit, squirted in some warm water, and amiably suggested, "Spit." Emerging from reverie—"it's too late," I said, "I swallowed."

What's the Psychosomatter With me?

Hypochondriacally inclined,
my aching back is in my mind;
The shooting pains my muscles mesh on
Show transference of repression;
Membrane swelling of the nose is
Evidence of more neurosis;
Puffy eyelids, rushy pulses,
Allergies, heat rash and ulcers,
Eczema, hay fever, warts;
Chronic feeling out of sorts,
Migraines, asthmas, hives and sinus
all add up to psychic minus.
Grandmamma was better off
with good old-fashioned whooping cough.

Flies Sleep

Flies sleep," he said, not exactly out of the clear sky. My cerebral sky was itself unclear, half-obliterated with sleep, so I said "Yes," in a friendly end-the-conversation sort of way, not feeling up to discussion or full-scale analysis.

I was, in fact, flirting deliciously with the threshold of consciousness, unwilling to go either way. Ahead lay peace and eiderdown oblivion; behind lay excitement and tension, and in between, fantasy and reality were playing those unscheduled games I love to watch.

During the afternoon we had opened doors and let in lots of flies. It had been a spectacular fall day, clean of summer's impurities, the sort of day that swings doors open involuntarily, inviting you to feel the crisp bite of truth waiting outside. This lets in hosts of flies, inviting you to feel their crisp bites also. They buzz and hover, cling and flit about, dart, dodge, defile and contaminate, and finally bite, swift nagging bites that set your nerves on edge. The thought of their sleeping is hilarious and unlikely, but I suppose they too must need their rest. Sleep and the world sleeps with you is a beautiful concept, in a class with white robes and harps and eternal harmony.

Flies sleep if he says so, but how can they, perched upside down on ceilings and walls, with unshutting many-faceted eyes. No matter, so long as they do. But why isn't our time their time for sleeping? Why can't they change back and forth from Standard to Daylight Saving to Standard the way we do? Why must they buzz around during my battles with insomnia? Don't they need their eight hours?

Well, he says that flies sleep, and this is the thought worth clinging to. It should make things easier for us all—yet sleep eludes me. Flies have bitten their way inside my brain and are buzzing all around the room, unable to quiet down. I try to soothe them with lullabies. "Flies sleep," I remind them. "Fold your little wings and settle down."

That's a pure and perfect declarative sentence ("Flies sleep", I mean). No nonsense—no ostentatious embellishment. A simple subject that even a three-year-old child would understand, and a simple verb that ditto. "Sleep,"—not a very active verb—in fact it denies the action promised by classroom definitions, yet it stimulates more mental activity than the verb "to run" as applied to Dick and Jane and Spot and Puff and Baby Sally. It's too stimulating. Combined with "flies", it's a positive curiosity piquer, and this is no time for curiosity piquing.

Flies sleep. See them sleep. Are they really asleep or are they pretending? Sh-h-h-h, Dick, sh-h-h Jane, don't wake up the little flies, let them sleep. When they wake up they will bite. They will bite you and me and Baby Sally, again and again.

It is late and I do not sleep. Time flies. Flies sleep, but not all flies. One fly flies. I do not sleep.

Sleep flies.

SECTION 7

Words to the Wise

Words to the Wise

Inside Pocket Story

L ucy Locket lost her pocket/Kitty Fisher found it." Remember that one? What was Mother Goose trying to tell us? A girl doesn't have pockets, and if she had had one, it would have been attached to her so how could she lose it?

Lucy's "pocket" must really have been one of those dainty ribbony dangle bags old-fashioned girls carry in Kate Greenaway illustrations. Notice, though, in following the plot through, that it was empty when Kitty found it. Lucy had been ripped off. The handbag situation was as bad then as now.

I know a woman who made herself a big wide skirt, and turned the hem over to the outside instead of under, sewing it vertically at six inch intervals to make a line of pockets all around. But, because she could never remember what she had put in which pocket, if she didn't have the skirt on straight, there was hell to pay trying to get oriented. Things fell out if she swished around too much, and stuff in the back pockets tended to get sat on.

But the effort goes to illustrate the frustration a woman can get into over yearning for a decent supply of pockets.

Pockets are the ultimate weapon of male chauvinism.

The cultural development of the pocket to its current peak of exquisite sophistication in menswear is one of the outstanding advances of mankind over womankind for his personal benefit. The outrageous mockery of pockets in women's clothes through the ages is socially medieval. Pockets, when she has them at all, are little dinky things hardly big enough for a snickersnee, often hidden in the seamline of a skirt, or opening vertically on her jacket so that the contents spill out faster than they went in. Never the deep safe flap pockets that men find routine equipment, although she may be lucky enough to get the flaps without the pockets. Never the roomy hip pockets that could generously accommodate a slim wallet or even a checkbook or an eyebrow pencil.

Sometimes, for the cute whimsy of it all, there will be an itsy bitsy pocket on the sleeve of a woman's trendy blouse (yes, really!), and since feminism has made a comeback, women's jeans often have a shallow pocket or two, but not the full measure of hip, side and watch pockets men get for the same price or less. And let's not be fooled. Men will not easily surrender these ill-gotten gains.

Sure, a woman gets along somehow. She sticks the car keys down her bosom, jams a few tissues up her sleeve, wedges her travelers checks into the waist of her pantyhose, holds the theatre tickets in her teeth if she doesn't have an escort, and then all she has to carry in her three extra hands is her money, makeup and glasses.

Women, you may have noticed, don't have much makeup or money anymore, and they save up for contact lenses. But what they do have is put into a contrivance some evil-minded male entrepreneur invented aeons ago on his way to becoming a millionaire, carelessly referred to as a purse.

Which, if it isn't stolen, gets lost.

Why does a woman lose her purse?

("Purse indeed! A purse is a little thing all crinkled together where it snaps open and shut, like someone with pursed lips. If you must have one, it should go inside of a pocketbook.)

O.K. then, why can't a woman ever find her pocketbook?

(Come on, now! "Pocketbook"! What book? What pocket?)

That's the whole point right there. What pocket? So why does a lady mislay her handbag? Because she doesn't have pockets. If she had pockets she wouldn't be bothered with a handbag, or pocketbook, and would pocket the silly purse if she had one, or exchange it for a wallet.

According to the latest statistics, there are more women's handbags lost daily than there are Canadian quarters found in U.S. slot machines in a given year. But according to the Feminist Conjectural Index, if men had to carry handbags, they would lose more than there are any kinds of quarters in U.S. slot machines. In Europe, a man with heavy fiscal responsibilities often does carry a handbag. It is a rectangular pouch with an ineffective-looking loop in one corner so that he can dangle it from his wrist (making him look ineffective and loopy). To a woman, it seems greedy to need all that and pockets too. In America, men who run out of pockets get into briefcases. Which, if they aren't stolen, get lost.

Today's Lucy, and Kitty too, looking for pockets, can go the transvestite route, as I have. There are men's and boys' jackets at your neighborhood thrift shops, and girls, would you believe three deep outside pockets and an inside pocket! If you run across any Harris tweeds in nice fall shades, I'm a 38 Short.

Personalized Preference

As I wove my way around the machinery in the print shop the other day, one of the men stopped me. He was standing by a job printing press which was going (in James Thurber's coinage) pocketa-pocketa-pocketa. He was about to feed a stack of high-quality super-soft paper napkins into the machine.

"Would you say," he asked me, "that the name and address should read from the corner of the napkin down toward the center or the other way around, reading down toward the corner?"

"Well, that's a good question," I said, stalling. I tried to reassemble myself as Emily Post Vanderbilt. "It depends," I mused, mentally patting a soignée coiffure with neatly gloved hand, "on how the napkin is to be put on the table. If you creased it diagonally and placed it at the left, plebeian fashion, you would have to twist sideways to read it in any case. If, on the other hand, you folded in the side corners, the personalized corner should head down, and you would want to read down toward that corner."

"O.K., down toward the corner. Let's go, boys." He began feeding. Personalized napkins plopped out of the other side of the press.

"On the other hand, I went on, "some people like to fold their napkins to look like pyramids or horns of plenty, with the points up. If this is the case, you will have put the names upside down."

"Look, you said down toward the corner. Now don't change your mind."

"Well, why did anyone want personalized paper napkins in the first place?" I asked crossly, trying to wriggle out of all responsibility.

"We get an order—we fill it. We don't ask why."

I moved on, disquieted. Why, I asked myself, why oh why does this particular hostess want personalized paper napkins? Monogrammed linen is one thing. Its usefulness and beauty last over the years. Besides, the monogram is usually illegible or meaningless. But to have one's name and address blatantly printed on paper napkins that will be used to mop a sloppy mouth or chin, then wadded up and chucked in the incinerator, seems less than decorous to me, and less than practical. If someone gives you his card you will, chances are, put it in your purse or wallet. You won't wipe your mouth with it and throw it away. You are doing yourself an indignity by personalizing your paper napkins. Next will be personalized Kleenex, paper towels, or worse.

Personalizing has certainly been enjoying a vogue. Even if you hate the very sight of your name and address, the mails will deliver you personalized pens and pencils, sample napkins, stickers and those key tags that are also miniature number plates. (If you drop your keys on the sidewalk the finder knows which car to steal!) My son comes home from college with personalized sheets, socks and underwear, none of them his. Personalized towels, linen, scarves, blouses, etc. are today a mail order catalogue must.

I don't mean to assume a critical sneer. Personalizing is a natural defense against society's regimentation. From our first howl to our last gasp society tries to assemble us into an orderly phalanx of ditto marks. We yearn to be personalized. When the I of identity first occurs to us we start writing our name all over school books and anything else handy. We write name and address, and hate to stop there, so we pad it, after Massachusetts, with U.S.A., Western Hemisphere, Earth, World, Universe, and our grandchildren may be able to draw it out much farther. We want to be pinpointed. We crave the knowledge that we are we and ours is ours, and not just part of the general turbulence.

This attitude may seem selfish—even anti-social. I say it is not anti-social, though it may be anti-socialistic. It isn't a feeling against anyone, but for the individual. It's against becoming ditto marks, not against other people and their marks, ditto or otherwise.

There is a catch, of course. The danger is that in following the drift toward personalization we are following a trend. To be effective as an individual we must shun trends. Trends are our undoing; we must be above them. We must personalize ourselves in some way other than by spreading our names all over the hardware and doilies. We should personalize our personalities.

Otherwise regimentation will conquer us regardless. Our personalization will eventually consist of just a number and we will all willy-nilly, go to the dog-tags.

Energy = My Cart Supercharged

My husband tells me that it takes a fantastic amount of energy, as represented by a number with a long, sinuous tail of zeros behind it, to make a small clod of matter. All that energy for a tiny clod. Makes you wonder. And it really threw me when I first heard that everything worth mentioning is made up of peppy little molecules zooming around day and night, never knocking off for a second. This is one of those scientific verities that defy the senses. Still there may be some truth in it. And then again, there may not. I'm not trying to start an argument.

Yesterday when I came out of the A & P with a shopping cart of groceries, I observed that my car was not where I left it. I had left it in one of the conventional slots painted on the parking lot. It was gone. Car theft by disorderly delinquent? Not at all. I glanced around and soon saw it sitting jauntily down toward the Pharmacy on an unslotted blacktop no-man's land some thirty yards from its former station. No-one had driven it; it just took off. A few minutes later as I walked into Backus & Soule, Dick Mulholland looked up and said. "Your car's moving. Betsy." He could see it sliding away again in back of me, out in the parking lot. It was docile enough when I pulled on the brake, but I certainly got the feeling that it was one of those restless days.

The clincher came later on when I was in the First National parking lot driving out the exit by the Atlantic gas station. I heard a clatter and rumble, and an unmanned shopping cart went careening past me, hell bent for GAR highway. I watched, frozen with fascination as it piled up against the curb and tipped over, its moment of glory dissipated.

Today when I was heading for the same exit, I was just in time for a repeat performance, only this time I didn't sit idly by. Instead, I lurched heroically from my car and went waddling after it in hot pursuit, hoping none of my friends were watching. I picked up a bit of speed as the grade steepened. but so did the cart. It was headed straight as an arrow for the intersection at Cross Road, with traffic looking as sprightly as it can for this time of year. I lunged forward, and caught it in the nick of time. Who knows what tragedy was thus averted? As I went panting back to my car you could see right away that it was trying to make up its mind whether to take off again or not.

One could get very fanciful about these hyper-animated vehicles. Is it the position of the stars or the phases of the moon that has them so supercharged? But that's not the point. The point is, what's going on here, and how long do we have to put up with it? Weren't we perhaps better off before e equaled mc squared? Or vice versa?

America The Beautiful

Perhaps one trouble with America is that she spends too much time in front of the mirror. She is too concerned with perfecting the physical image reflected there, and too unconcerned over the heart and soul.

She is a fine physical specimen, sleek, well-fed, well-dressed, but no amount of makeup can hide a twitching around the mouth and a nervous restlessness in the eyes. The glass reflects affluence and success—a well-groomed figure, but the eyes turn back again for reassurance, for they see they have lost their young fire, and are frightened.

It was heart and soul, not beauty, that won freedom and fought for democracy. We have been spoiled by the spoils of those wars. We inherited freedom already paid for, and like anything easily come by, its value was partly forgotten. When we dissipate our legacy it is gone.

Freedom is not free. It is the most expensive thing we own, and worth more than we can pay. It requires more of us than our jobs, more than all our efforts to make our country rich and strong and generous. It requires full-time dedicated responsibility of everyone who accepts it.

When the world sees us it is not fooled by the rich, beautiful facade that we admire so much in the glass. It looks in our eyes for the fire that was once there. Until we turn away from the mirror and look back at the world, rekindled, our image will never be worth reflecting.

Holidays

Holidays

My Pet Christmas

What do you want for Xmas this year? We always like to specialize—it simplifies planning and sometimes we get a price break with bulk shipment. Let's see, was last year going to be artifacts-ordered-from-museum-catalogs year, only we never got the order out on time? And the year before, some Cape author we like very much got out a book at just the right moment, priced right for our budget...and the year before that...was that the magazine subscription year, or the year of the stretch socks? Another year, it seems to me, we had Asian flu and felt this was an excuse to let last minute drug store items commemorate the glad tidings. I don't mean to belittle drug store items, believe me. Without them Christmas wouldn't be Christmas, and I'm not kidding. But the fact is that ordinarily one is expected to go farther afield than the drug store, for outside-the-family presents anyway.

Ideally one finds a unique little boutique in some out-of-the way spot (it needn't be Europe, really). The corner of an alley not far from the river is a good location. One stumbles down worn stone steps into a courtyard alive with flowers. Just off the courtyard, below street level is the shop, undiscovered save by the natives. It has no obtrusive sign (natives know where it is), and all that distinguishes it from the native dwellings surrounding it are a couple of priceless objects in the window. Inside the natives are busy at their native craft, which happens to be to produce both a decorative and useful item that will excite all one's friends, and which they need but don't realize they need until they unwrap it Xmas day. Then they know they will never be without it. It is handhewn and custom-stitched from native-grown materials, and was bought for only a fraction of its worth, but still costs enough to be respectable. And though it may not be personalized, one must remember that there are no two exactly alike.

This is all as it should be, and it should be awfully nice and fun and time consuming. Actually the Cape is good at this type of thing, but it seems unimaginative to go around discovering shops next door. Still, in the interest of patronizing local industry, I recommend it.

But as for me, I think this is going to be my "pet" year. I'm going to give away pets. Oh, I've known desperate housewives to unload litters of kittens on distant relatives with all the philanthropy of the Greeks bearing Trojan horses, but this isn't quite what I have in mind. That everyone should have a pet is an accepted part of the American way of life, yet I know quite a few people who don't at the moment have any pets at all, and others who have room for more. Now, I'm in a particularly good position to give away pets. My children have grown up and flown the nest, but they have left their pets behind and their pets in some cases have produced other pets, so we honestly have more pets than we actually need. But I'm not talking about the cats. I'm going to give away all kinds of pets except cats. Who gets which will, of coarse, be determined by my friends' personalities and closeness. An abbreviated list of the choice of delicacies would include guinea pigs, parakeets, horses, a siberian husky, and always available for those forgotten people on the list are some hamsters and an occasional turtle.

What appeals to me about this scheme is that the capital outlay has already been made, and all I have to worry about is wrapping and shipping. But why wrap and ship? Why doesn't everyone just come down and pick up their own. We love to have friends come around in holiday season. Bring your own bottle, and we'll provide you with a week's supply of dog food or birdseed, as the case may be.

Twelve Years of Christmas

Although we have yet to make Peace on Earth a tradition, its chances always seem a lot brighter at Christmas, when traditions are particularly honored. For Peace (that battered ensign) is sanctified by the Heavenly Host at Christmas, whatever holocaust lurks without. It is traditional that this be so.

We always hoped to instill a deep sense of tradition in the family at Christmas, and with due modesty I must admit that at times our success went beyond our wildest dreams. All we really expected was to capture a moment or two of recognizable uniformity amid unordered chaos in which to pay homage to certain rites. Hanging stockings together above the hearth, for example, seemed to be a Yuletide activity for which we should all be able to assemble with singleness of purpose. Opening them next morning, ditto. The ritual of tree selecting, cutting and decorating was another priority happening that might be called on to become traditional. And so on.

In this way the first twelve years passed with cooperation and appropriate enthusiasm from the children, who recognized a season of opportunity and good will when they saw one.

The next twelve years, however, saw a new spirit entering the proceedings that gave a plump comfortable spirit of tradition wild vitality and mushroom growth. The children, now began to realize that what made for much of the cheer and hilarity were, in fact, traditions, however inane, and also that getting in on the Santa Claus act had some often humorous advantages. From then on the lid was off. Traditions sprouted like crabgrass. Almost every thing we did one year had to be repeated the next year with embellishments. The following year it was engraved into family law and lore.

We had traditional ways of doing everything while playing traditional music and drinking traditional beverages. We read traditional Christmas stories aloud in front of a traditional fire with each family member recognizing a traditional seating arrangement. We lighted candles in all the windows (and we live in a glass house) at a traditional time on Christmas Eve and went galloping around outside with shouts of appreciation, snow or rain, to admire them (since we live too far out for neighbors' appreciation).

Because my husband and I were procrastinating last minute shoppers, our Christmas Eve forays to the stores became a tradition. To be forehanded one year would have been an outrage. Over these next twelve years we were kept firmly in our place by our progeny, who would not countenance our being anywhere but in Orleans the night before Christmas, closing down H.H. Snow's, and Livingston's, winding up for a cup of cheer at Backus and Soule's. After that, came reading the Christmas Carol and reciting The Night Before Christmas from memory prompted by children while the birthday size candles burned down on the tiny Christmas tree. There was then a traditional drinking of eggnog, the candles in every window ceremony, and at 11:45 we all lurched out into the cold to go to a midnight service. Santa Claus then had from say 1-3am to do his bit. After that various alarm clocks went off at 4, 5 or 6 so that various members of the family could add a fillip of surprise and imagination to Santa's exploits. And so on into that ceremonial of ceremonials, Christmas Day. Here from 8 A.M. until 10 at night every moment was accounted for in traditional activity.

On the twelfth year of the second twelve years we went through so many traditional activities in the twelve days of Christmas that it was like a steeplechase, racing from hurdle to hurdle. We went through it all hysterically determined to leave no tradition unturned. When it was over we looked and said, "Really!"

One of our daughters said, "Next Christmas we've got to get off this production line and back to simplicity. Next year let's make each other's presents and keep everything absolutely basic."

So now we have a new tradition—making each other's presents.

But in fact we are saved by another belle. Our oldest son married. Now his children start the cycles anew.

Which is as good an excuse as I can imagine to settle your brains for a long winter's nap. Happy Christmas to all, and to all a Good Night!

The Good Old Days

Christmas is a time when we hark back. We may hark back farther than you—we don't know—but in any case you must agree that Things Have Changed.

In our day there wasn't all this electric light hoopla. We put real candles in the windows and very delicate shiny balls on the tree. Our presents were all done up in white tissue paper with real red ribbon, and the name written in crayon on the outside.

We didn't have rubber or plastic Betsy Wetsy dolls, or Walky-Talky dolls: The doll we got one Christmas when we were seven was a real doll made of something like plaster of Paris, with arms and legs that hooked to an elastic inside and eyes that blinked open and shut. Her clothes that came in a little steamer trunk were pinafores, petticoats and rompers and a navy blue velvet dress with a lace collar exactly like one of our own, and were all tenderly sewn for us by our Aunt Ellen and Aunt Ruth whose bounty knew no bounds.

We had mighty fine electric trains in our day too (and don't you kids forget it) but we didn't have as many gidgets and gadgets, switches and swatches. Everything was so much simpler, and, if we do say so, better, for those were the Good Old Days.

We didn't have all these parties, at school, at church, scouts, clubs, bring a 10¢ gift, a 25¢ gift, a 50¢ gift. Things certainly have changed. Santa Claus is a dime a dozen now, on every street corner, in every shop, arriving by plane or helicopter. In our day he was a "jolly old elf" and we never actually saw him, although if we woke in the night we sometimes heard strange sounds, and at the window between the swirls of snow (in our day it always snowed) we might catch the moment when "away they all flew like the down of a thistle."

But we remember our mother saying even then, "This year we must keep everything simpler," and quoting whoever it was that said so cogently, "Christmas has us by the throat again!" She was remembering her Good Old Days, her doll with the stuffed body and china head—days when sleighs and sleighbells were the natural order of a winter's day.

So who are we to distinguish between the store Santa Clauses and the traditional St. Nick, between what we had and what they have, so long as, with the turn of a music box key or the distant sound of carollers, with the wonder a doll brings to a little girl whether it is made of plastic or papier maché, the magic is recaptured. So long as the church pageant is The Nativity to her, it is to us too.

These are her Good Old Days. Let's make them better than ever, for she knows better than we the difference between the tinsel and the Star.

The Guilt-Framed Mirror

Time to pack the tinsel balls;
Holly boughs are looking wilty.
Come, ye faithful—check the hauls;
'Tis the season to feel guilty.

Come now, you've been feeling guilty just like everyone else. None escape. No one can be above it all. If the presents don't get you, the parties will. If the bills don't get you, the charities will. Take the simple routine of giving presents: If you give too little, you feel mean;—too much, you're profligate;—nothing at all—you should be shot. The question isn't whether to feel guilty, but which kind of guilt you want to settle for.

If you're a housewife you have felt over the holidays more conscious than ever of your role as physical and spiritual provider. How did the cookies turn out—or didn't you make any? Fruitcake this year, or not? Was the house attractive or a mess? Were you happy and cheerful as you went about your busy chores? Did you remember all those strange relatives you married into? And how about the milkman and paper boy and everyone else who does you good service? Did the batch of cards you sent weigh in as heavily as those you received? Did you look on those who forgot you with divine forgiveness?

If you're a man, you must feel pretty terrible for not coming across as handsomely as last year—or if you did, you shouldn't be so smug about it. While the women were in the kitchen making all those goodies, you might at least have been laying the fire or paying bills or something instead of lounging on the end of your spine watching TV. Too bad you didn't help with the cards this year. You might at least have done your friends. That was quite a hangover you had Saturday, when the children wanted you to help with the tree.

How did you all feel when Uncle Whosis sent that unexpected check? Guilty, that's how you felt. All the perfumes of Arabia, or years of psychotherapy will not sweeten your conscience, for a few days, anyway.

There are ways, of course, of deadening the pain somewhat. There is the highly developed rationalizing mechanism that churns

147

out excuses as steadily as the guilt germs collect. "Of course they gave more than we did. With his income. . ." "No one in the house does any work but me, so what can anyone expect," or "Considering all our responsibilities and how hard we work, it's amazing that we get anything done at all around Christmas time. . ." This is like taking aspirin for a cold. It makes you feel better, but can't be called a cure.

Then there is the escape hatch, or "Stay me with flagons" method, which needs no explanation. You simply pick your favorite opiate or hallucinogen and stay with it until the danger is well past. This is like taking whiskey for a cold.

One of the most effective methods for women, though, is Guilting the Lily. What they do is to look around them and find the person (invariably another woman) who does everything that should be done to perfection and is the envy of all. She gets her cards out by December 15th, having already sent several packages to friends and our boys overseas. She makes her own cookies, and pies, and fruitcake by old family recipes. She gives attractive, useful, handmade presents to her family, gifts to the needy, successful liquor-free parties for teenagers, and all on savings she had set aside for the purpose. She is the lily, and through dark implications you must guilt her. "Yes, I admit she's marvelous," you say, "but something has to give. . . her children, you know. . ." or "If she spent as much time on her personality as she does on cookie batter. . ." or "Thank God my feelings of inadequacy and insecurity don't affect me THAT way. . ."

And all of a sudden you feel well again. Happy New Year!

Another Mother's Day

A nother Mother's Day has been batted over the fence, the day the merchandisers set aside for Everyman to make a home run and promote the sale of sentimental bats and balls. It was a merchandising masterstroke. So many of us have mothers or are them. Few get through the sunny Sunday unscathed. It's rude to object to Mother's Day, unless you are a mother and your own is out of hearing, and in such a case it's looking a potential gift horse in the mouth. There are ways of getting out of it with a little fancy footwork, but such a course is fraught with danger. Few succeed.

"Did you send your mother some flowers?" my husband was asked by one of his students last Sunday.

"My mother? Flowers? Why?" He looked startled.

"It's Mother's Day, Mr. Cochran."

"Oh that. Oh well, I don't believe in Mother's Day," he said ingenuously, laying his pitiful cards on the table.

"Mr. Cochran! Don't you think mothers deserve to have this one teeny little day in the whole year just for them? You ought to be ashamed!"

By this time he had regained his debonair aplomb, "Why every day is Mother's Day to me. You may be nice to your mother once a year, but I'm nice to mine every day."

"Flowers every day?"

"Flowers, candy, perfume, cards—you name it." he said, laying it on thick and getting in deeper...

Now this is the sort of footwork that could trip you up but I record it as a good try.

Actually, if you feel at all kindly toward your mother, the loveliest thing you can do for her is to give her a little rest. I have yet to know a mother who thinks she gets enough sleep. Mothers are notorious insomniacs. After a full day of housework, chauffeuring and nagging, a mother falls into bed, but sleep is denied her. She hears noises. Children, dogs, cats, clocks ticking, robbers breaking and entering, and thoughts of the next day's duties intrude on her slumber. Dawn finds her in her bathrobe sitting in the living room petulantly reading the Readers Digest. No wonder she's always in such a nasty humor. She never gets enough sleep.

Last Sunday, after staggering through my maternal chores heavy-lidded, I decided, during a lull in the afternoon, that I owed it to myself to take a nap, so I went purposefully to bed. Just as my cerebrations were beginning to lose their continuity, the telephone rang. I lifted the receiver to stop the horrid noise.

"Happy Mother's Day!" said the voice of another mother who was once my friend. "You're the most mother mother I know," she went on, "so I just wanted to wish you a happy day."

"Thanks," I said. "I've had it. Same to you."

I only mention this to prove my point. Sleep is the sweetest thing a mother can have. Sleep is what she wants on Mother's Day. Don't call her up. Don't come around with candy and flowers. Leave her alone. Commend her to the arms of Morpheus. It's the kindest thing you can do for the old girl.

How's that for footwork?

Pot Pourri

Pot Pourri

The Day I Ran The Bermuda Triangle

March 31, 1985: I can still hear the awed hush of the multitude as I burst into the police recreation stadium after rounding the final point of the triangular course—the only woman to run the mile in 11:38 minutes that day in Bermuda. And as the triumph is bruited abroad I can visualize my husband, somewhat distraught, dishing out a "happy buck" at the Orleans Rotary Club because his Rotary Ann finished the mile a full half hour ahead of him (he started later). But I'm getting ahead of my story.

It was at the VanderMay Suite in the Sonesta Beach Hotel that the initial plans were laid to make a Lower Cape sweep of the Bermuda Mile Challenge. Revelers present were participants in the second annual Orleans Rotary sojourn to Bermuda and were feeling no pain—yet. Judy Scofield, of Orleans and Yarmouthport, came up with a fistful of flyers describing the race, which was to benefit police projects for Bermuda youth, and her fanatic enthusiasm was not to be denied. Seven of us signed up before the second drink was poured—she was that persuasive. I did not sign up. I was engaged in an intellectual conversation in another corner of the suite, but my husband signed up for me, giving me the beady eyeball across the crowded room. "It's just one mile," he pointed out later. "You'll never get a chance like that again."

I put it out of my mind. Something would come up. Tornado. A fractured tibia. Cardiac arrest. I didn't even worry about what to wear, I was so sure of a last minute reprieve.

Occasionally, during the next few days, tour companions would make oblique references to the impending challenge, betraying anxious thoughts on my behalf. "Have you ever actually jogged a mile before?" for instance, and "You don't have to run, you know. It would be O.K. to walk. I mean, there'll be so many people in the race, who's to notice what you do? I bet you could even pull a Rosie Ruiz and get away with it." I mentally stored that last suggestion near the top of the pile.

Three of our candidates escaped somehow. One impaled his bare foot on a spike of coral, eliciting genuine sympathy. The other two abandoned the team (or saw the light) for other reasons. This left three women (Judy, Mary VanderMay and me) for the women's race, and one man (my husband) for the men's, to uphold the honor of the Cape and Rotary International.

I don't know what Judy was up to during the days before the race, but she emerged leaner, tanner and more rippling of muscle at each evening's get-together at the VanderMay Suite. Mary too was turning a rich mahogany and was glowing with health and vitality as the days went by after limbering up visits to the Sonesta Beach Spa. They would both do us proud, I knew. My approach was to rest up for the ordeal without actually taking to my bed. I went on relaxing bus and taxi rides from one end of the island to the other, and sauntered lazily through Hamilton shops and the Botanical Gardens, refueling myself generously at lunchtime with local delicacies even though I knew there would be five course Sonesta dinners awaiting later on.

I was still counting on providential intervention. In my more lucid moments I knew a tornado was highly unlikely, but put faith in a torrential downpour or an opportune migraine.

The day, Sunday, dawned gusty and cloudy, but cleared up as moments ticked ominously by. I waded through the wardrobe but couldn't come up with any running shorts, T-shirt or my trusty New Balance running shoes. Would that wash as an excuse? Probably not. I did have my Nauset Sports "Pony" sneakers with velcro tabs, and my Bradlee's chinos, and contenders were all being given free T-shirts with "Malibu Coconut Rum" emblazened across the bosom, so there was no way I could claim to be inadequately clothed. I also managed to dig out a visor hat of my husband's with "Boston Marathon" written across the front, for an authentic touch.

It was too late now to cop out. We lingerers had to shoulder the burden. The ladies ran at 11 am and the men at 11:30. I had to focus on not being overtaken by the men's race. Where was this enormous crowd everyone talked about that I could hide in? There were just 36 of us. The hour approached. I took off my glasses, pulled down my visor and set my jaw. I hunted blindly for the starting line. Judy was jogging gently in place to limber up, and

Mary was doing stretching exercises. They both looked cool and agile, and made supportive and encouraging remarks. When the gun went off I had to persuade Mary not to stay back and help me through, but after I convinced her to spurt on ahead with the rest, both she and Judy finished very creditably, and all 35 disappeared from my sight in two seconds flat.

There was a long roller-coaster downhill plunge to begin with, followed by an uphill just when you were getting short of breath. I hummed a prayerful spiritual to my cardio-vascular system as we lumbered along together.

It was, as I have said, a triangular course, so this was my chance to try the Rosie Ruiz ploy, cut out around and back, and appear triumphantly ahead of the pack, but I couldn't see well enough to do it without my glasses, and the police had thoughtfully stationed helpers every quarter mile to encourage us on our way. The street was more or less lined with cheering spectators who could spot any defection. I plodded on.

Mary and Judy jogged back to accompany me in my stadium entrance. The rest is history. Cool water passed my parched lips and I knew that my peak experience was all over but the shouting.

There was a lump in my throat as I turned in my number (177). Then a quick change into civvies in the ladies' room, and I was once more an incognito spectator, sipping a free sample of Malibu coconut rum laced with pineapple juice, watching my husband finish the men's race with his usual insouciance.

Now, back home, I find that every time I pull on my chinos and Pony velcro-tabbed sneakers it is with a new feeling of reverence. (The Malibu shirt shrank almost out of sight with the first washing). But I gave the Boston Marathon hat back to my husband on the firm understanding that he keep his beady eyeballs to himself from now on.

To S.C. on His Birthday, 1964

Many Happy Returns, pop, and love—Bets.

And did he hear the Sirens' song?
And did he find the Golden Fleece?
And did my father walk among
Olympians, on the Isles of Greece?
This year's Odysseus (né S.C.)
in challenging Hellenic portals,
strolling with Penelope
through the gardens of immortals
sees the attic shapes entire
within the mind—ah, what a way
to keep alive the Delphic fire
and celebrate a natal day!

Making Soap

Strictly speaking, harvesting the fat of the Narrow Land should somehow include fat—from nuts, perhaps, or (not too strictly speaking), bayberries. "Today," says Euell Gibbons in *Stalking the Blue-eyed Scallop,* "Bayberries are best known for the fragrant, green candles made of their wax and commonly sold in quaint little gift shops all over Cape Cod. To our ancestors, the bayberry bush was not only a source of candles...but it was also a medicinal herb—a dye plant, and a kitchen herb or spice; the wax was used as an aid to ironing clothes and as an ingredient of homemade soap...When soap-making was a universally practiced household art, the housewives along the Atlantic shore had in the Bayberry a never-failing source of 'soap grease,' for Bayberry wax will saponify like fat."

Today on the Cape you may still occasionally encounter bayberries done up in calico for waxing the bottom of irons to make them glide smoothly. You may also find an occasional ambitious soul who will collect the vast quantities of tiny gray berries necessary to render enough wax to pour into a candle mold or drip on a wick—but not often. And *who* makes *soap* nowadays?

Granny Cochran does. Not of bayberries, to be sure, (though no doubt she'd be willing if you'd bring her the wax), but every fall when the days get crisp Mrs. Moncrieff Cochran of Pleasant Bay Narrows in South Orleans gets out the big enamel kettles and pans, and brings in the cans of leftover fat from the shed, for her fall soap-making.

"First you have to clean out the ice-chest, to make room," said Mrs. Cochran, who counts among her many achievements her age—90; her grandchildren—23; and her great-grandchildren—7. She has been making soap, usually twice a year, for quite some time now. "My aunt told my mother how to do it...It's really very simple. There's not much to it...We always used the receipt on the Babbitt Lye cans, but they don't print it there anymore. Now if you want to know how to do it you have to send for directions."

She measured out her fat by pouring it from the assorted

containers surrounding her into a can which she then dumped into a large kettle. The fat she uses is whatever has accumulated from cooking over the summer, along with some that friends have brought.

"Any kind of fat at all will do, no matter how mildewed it is," she said, "though I like it as pure as possible. Lamb fat makes the hardest soap. Our ancestors used to make tallow candles out of lamb fat."

After measuring the fat she put in twice as much water, and carried the kettle over to the stove. "Now that has to boil for 20 minutes or so," she said. ".....I dropped some last year. It was like skating around on molasses until we had cleaned it all up."

She looked around for another kettle she could spare from her jelly-making (that was going on almost simultaneously)—finally found one and started another lot of fat and water to boil. Then, a cup of tea with us while the boiling was going on, after which the fat was allowed to cool and finally to chill to a hard crust in the refrigerator.

Two days later, after the fat had hardened, she took it out, scraped off whatever residue clung to the bottom and weighed it.

"Nine and a quarter pounds.....subtract three and a quarter— there, that's enough. Now I've got to get my hands icky again."

Six pounds of fat combine with one can of Babbitt's Lye mixed with 1 quart and a cup of water (two and a half pints of water, to put it another way) to make the right proportions for soap. She poured the can of lye into an enamel pitcher of measured water. It soon began to steam as the chemical reaction generated heat. "It gets boiling hot...No wonder it cleans drains," she said. The pitcher felt hot to the touch. In the meantime the six pounds of fat was warming on the stove. "They both have to be blood heat," she said. When the fat had heated to about 100° and the lye and water cooled to about 100° they were combined in an enamel kettle (aluminum would react with the lye), and stirred for ten or fifteen minutes.

The liquid soap was then poured out into enamel pans and left undisturbed for two more days. By this time it had reached the right consistency to be cut into cakes.

There was, in addition to the practical benefits, a real aesthetic satisfaction derived from turning something as slimy, smelly and unattractive as leftover fat into clean pure odorless soap. And what is the soap like? From experience we know it to be a fine, substantial, pure cleaning agent. It lathers well. It's easy on the hands. We heard one story about a lady who got a rash from Ivory that cleared up when she started using Granny's soap. But, the story went on, there was another lady who claimed she got a rash from Granny's soap, or so Granny said. We use it in the bathroom and grate it for washing dishes at the kitchen sink (or put scraps in a soap saver).

Does Mrs. Cochran use it for her bathroom soap as well as in the kitchen? "I get Pears Soap for my own personal use because we always have, and I don't change," she said. "I get the transparent, unscented kind."

We remembered a saying she has often quoted at such appropriate moments "Sweetest, she who smells of naught!"

The Keeper of the Files

I've been asked to whip up some sort of chronology of *The Cape Codder's* 50 years, highlighting whatever the paper highlighted— not an unreasonable request, since I've been here so long and happen to be in charge of the files. But there are a couple of problems.

The files of the early years consist of huge bound volumes, each one weighing a ton, and when I get one off the shelf I can't get it back up again. So they fill the office and I can't get at my desk. Yet to fall back on my memory, a very slippery trip, breaks all the cardinal rules, like: don't be personal, be objective and be sure you get your facts straight.

But not to write anything is like turning your back on your best friend.

Jack and Laura Johnson invited us to Truro shortly after they gave birth to *The Cape Codder.* Jack had hired my husband, Mon Cochran, to help collect advertisements. We had just moved to the Cape, so it was still new to me, and I was profoundly awed by the cliffs beyond Longnook Road where they lived, which of course would become part of the National Seashore 20 years later. I actually wrote a sonnet about them 10 years later that Malcolm Hobbs printed in 1957. *The Cape Codder* during the late '40s, however, was only of peripheral interest to me as I was heavily involved with five small children.

During the '50s, though, when the new *Cape Codder* building was completed, I joined the staff part-time, and got to edit several of those great old columns: "My Pamet"; "Strictly For The Birds"; "Six Miles Square"; "Orleans Scenes"; and Herb Fuller's weather rundown of the previous week. I met our future cartoonist Gordon Brooks when Peggy Hobbs and I interviewed him for an article on his silk screening. Peggy took the pictures, and soon became a prize-winning photographer for the paper. Vernon Smith, another great friend of the paper's, designed the front page flag and made the sign for the new building.

Overdevelopment of the Cape was becoming a serious issue. Schools were beginning to get crowded, with the threat of the baby boomers looming. Snow Library burned down during a heavy winter storm in the early '50s. Ponds were frozen and the fire trucks couldn't save it. Irreplaceable town records were lost, but the tragedy stirred the town to rally and support the building of a new up-to-date library at its present site.

Politically, the Cape was solidly Republican in those days. The only two noticeable Democrats in Orleans were said to be Gaston Norgeot and Orin Tovrov. *The Cape Codder's* support went to individuals rather than any party choice.

The idea of a National Seashore started in the '50s and came to fruition in the '60s. I got my first assignment as a reporter covering the Eastham Citizen's Committee's dissenting meetings.

Mon Cochran left *The Cape Codder* in 1947 when he was asked by the Orleans School Investigating Committee to teach science at the high school for the final six weeks. Several teachers had left that year because the boys (who grew up with their fathers away during World War II) were so hard to handle.

Mon found he liked teaching, and was asked to stay on, and later became the school's first full-time guidance director. The concept of guidance in public schools was relatively new, and in the early '60s his authority was challenged by the school principal, Armand Guarino, and the school superintendent, Sidney Pierce. The resulting fracas, which included several public hearings in the high school auditorium, was covered in detail by *The Cape Codder.* The National Education Association came to Mon's rescue, and the case was finally settled out of court. He resigned, and shortly afterward we joined two other couples to revive Sea Pines School in Brewster as an independent high school.

I taught ninth grade English at Sea Pines that year, and my only direct connection with *The Cape Codder* was as a columnist. We were involved with Sea Pines School from 1962 to 1972, when it had to close for lack of funds. But the '60s were a very lively time for the paper, and a big growth period. In October 1964, Malcolm Hobbs and his wife, Gwen, were invited to join a People to People Goodwill tour made by New England newspaper editors to communist countries, the first newspeople to be admitted after Stalin's death. "We made 19 flights in 21 days," Gwen told me.

On the Cape the pace seemed to be quickened every year. Schools eventually regionalized, with a few notable exceptions. Zoning was a constant issue, as of course were the problems that arose in connection with the Seashore. Scout groups became more and more active, storms made big news every year or so, malls sprouted around the Cape like mushrooms, theatrical groups came and went, and some put down roots. Gwen and I did "Focus" feature stories from 1970-80; she took some superb pictures, while I did the text. Sea Pines Abroad in Austria, an offshoot of Sea Pines in Brewster, occupied me for several months each year until 1987.

By 1988 I was back at a desk at *The Cape Codder,* looking around for a typewriter and not finding one. John Ullman says I can use his, but I know a sacred icon when I see it.

Our bound volumes end with 1983, but my clipping files go back that far, and we do have a big temperamental microfilm machine, so feel free to come in and find what you're looking for.

Because right now my deadline has me by the throat. And *The Cape Codder's* on a roll.

We Mourn the Man, and Honor His Legacy

Now, nine months after the death of Malcolm Hobbs, we are more than ever aware of his legacy. Lest we forget, readers remind us. His fine sense of language, his careful editing, his understanding of small community needs while seeing global implications, his humor, his bullshit intolerance all went into making a unique newspaper with a devoted following.

After handing over the ownership of the paper in 1990, Malcolm went right on coming to the office daily, writing editorials, giving advice and telling John Ullman where to get off. He continued this year after year until this past spring.

His death on March 15 was a painful blow to *The Cape Codder,* bringing a sense of parental loss, along with losing a friend and mentor, to many who had worked with him over the years.

From 1951 to 1990 he owned the paper, was editor and publisher; and no one ever had to wonder who was boss or where the buck stopped. But he was a benevolent despot, with a rare sense of humor. He hated to fire anyone and rarely did. Yet he knew his first duty was to strive for perfection in putting out his paper.

When he bought the fledgling newspaper from Jack Johnson, Malcolm became the owner of "a paper with few readers, fewer subscriptions, but an unbeatable name," John Ullman later wrote. Before long it was flourishing. Subscriptions and circulation soared, on Cape and off. Malcolm wasn't one to kowtow to advertisers, but managed to draw them in readily because they knew he had the readership they needed. In the early 1960s the subscriber list was around 3,500 and 30 years later it has quadrupled.

He told his reporters to make stories readable from the first paragraph, pertinent to trends, and informed beyond the surface. "In the end, what it boils down to is style," he said... "How the colors are arranged distinguishes the painter from the dauber." It was good advice, and it paid off.

Malcolm's editorial stands were unequivocal and courageous. He was more likely to tackle an issue than an individual, and the issue he is most remembered for was his support for establishing the Cape Cod National Seashore. The Seashore's Salt Pond Visitor Center hosted his memorial service, which included remarks by Jonathan Moore, Francis Sargent, John Hay, Tony Kahn (for his father, E.J. Kahn), and Congressman Gerry Studds along with those of staff members and his son Christopher.

News of his death brought waves of letters from readers in the ensuing weeks, expressing deep appreciation widely felt. Words that cropped up again and again were: commitment, loyalty, feisty, principles, and, of course, curmudgeon. A common thread running through many letters, and expressed in the report made by his successor, Greg O'Brien, was that Malcolm represented a vanishing breed and era. Times have changed, and newspaper production with them. But it was his character and personality that got top billing every time.

"Malcolm Hobbs was very much like quahog pie," wrote John Ullman, his great friend, "lots of crust, but warm and satisfying inside."

And from Josephine Del Deo: "Mal, the house lights are up; the audience is on its feet. I hope you can hear that endless wave of applause as you take your final curtain call."

In the Eye of the Beholder

In the Eye of the Beholder

A Bargain's a Bargain

A bargain is to me as drink to the thirsty, food to the glutton and an axe to a tree. I am defenseless.

The bargains that have felled me over the ages would fill a warehouse, though the dump has more often claimed them. The only way I can survive a Sears Roebuck catalog unscathed is by studying it in such detail that I grow drowsy with intoxication at last, and sleep it off. Often, though, I find I have sent for something before giving myself time to sober up. This happened in the case of the room-divider-book-case whose poles were too short for the room, and which lay unassembled in the corner for six months or more, its springs, screws and washers tossed loosely into a torn carton, its shelves lying unvarnished and neglected except for one part of the guinea pig cage.

It happened, too, about a month ago, on a gloomy day when the Sears catalog was the one delirious touch of color I could find around the house. Before I knew what was happening I was hooked by a yellow jumper and print blouse, designed to be worn together or separately. Price—$6.66—plus postage, of course. The jumper was one of those A-line not-what-you-might-call-form-fitting shifts. How very In, I thought. The blouse was—well—a blouse. I ordered the combination a size larger than I usually wear on the theory that cheap clothes tend to be skimpy. You get more material for your money that way too.

In due course, it came. Due course for Sears is seldom more than a week. Sometimes I wish it were longer. I tore open the crude brown paper wrappings bravely. The jumper was yellow all right. Perfect for wearing along a dark street at night. The blouse was—well—a blouse—one whose buttons were affixed with a single tenuous thread.

I slipped into the ensemble for my daughter's appraisal. In one respect I had certainly scored. It wasn't skimpy. The blouse allowed real freedom of action. The jumper draped itself around me like a parachute that has done its duty and come gracefully to rest. From the front I had a Halloween aspect, as if turned out in an electric pumpkin-colored ghost costume. Side-view I suggested a gaff-rigged catboat trying to come about in the light air of the sunset hour.

"I know it isn't supposed to cling, mother, but couldn't you do something to suggest a waistline?"

"I think it's *supposed* to look like this."

"Well, if that's the way you *want* it. But it's way too long and makes you look fat."

So something had to be done, and of course the most effective way to keep a bargain a bargain is to do whatever requires the least amount of effort. I scrutinized the jumper carefully and decided that the simplest improvement I could make would be to remove the two fake pocket flaps that broke the A-line sweep in front. It only required a couple of minutes with a pair of scissors. But it revealed four little holes that the cutters had made to line up the pocket flaps for the seamstresses. How to disguise them? Long experience with the devastation of cigarette ashes has made me resourceful. Clipping little round patches from the facing, I plugged the holes from the back with the help of iron-on tape. But the material was too thin and the tape showed through, so I removed it, and laboriously unraveled bits of thread from the seams (which luckily were not pinked), and darned the holes, with delicacy and patience. This was better. Now they just looked like places where I had been caught on a nail. But the jumper was still too long and baggy. After three pin-ups I achieved what I felt to be knee-cap-line perfection, and awaited my daughter's approval.

"It's *O.K.,* but you still look fat, mother. Face it, you should have bought a smaller size."

Well, after buying some matching yellow thread and oiling the machine, all I had to do was take a nip in each of the six seams. When I tried it on again, it fit much better, but had grown dingy from being worked over, and after all that nipping it was now too short, so I let the hem down again, and washed it. It ran a little in the wash and lost some of its body and crispness.

But for $6.66 plus postage and 15¢ for thread, I'm still ahead in the spring wardrobe game, and my goodness, the material alone must have been worth...but I musn't forget to strengthen the sewing on those blouse buttons.

Now I can outshine a May-pole in my ready-to-wear day-glow saffron tent. And to be sure it's legal, I'm applying to the zoning appeals board for a variance.

◗

Why Pan Dowdy?

Sophia Loren gives the new dowdy look the good streetwear swagger of approval. Why pan it? Jacqueline Onassis can't wait to get into the longer skirts. Why must the lady be kept waiting? Sure, we know there are a lot of lecherous old meat auction addicts who bid for leg of lamb even over breast of chicken, but we can turn them loose at "Oh, Calcutta," where they can worship their sacred cows on the hoof, and let the rest of us chicks support the garment industry while there still is one.

What's more, among women's rights used to be the right to look dowdy when she was middle-aged. Back in another half-century, women had the right to grow up. If Women's Lib can't restore these privileges, I'm easing up on my demonstrating, and urging my friends to do the same. You can't blame a woman for taking to the bottle if she has to wander around looking like an infant all her life.

It's exciting to think of the wide world of adult clothing we can reintroduce ourselves to. Think of the grown-up styles and shapes that haven't been touched by manufacturers for years. All this time we've been dressing for the journey back to the womb, and we've gone the whole way, from pinafores to jumpers to smocks and shifts (euphemisms for baby's nighties), to topless bikinis (euphemisms for diapers or bellybands), arriving inevitably at the birthday suit. Well now, happy birthday suit to you. Personally, I'm glad to turn around and grab a ride back. I'm up in the attic already, pulling out the good old stuff we used to wear when women were women, and lots of kids wished they were too. Remember all the beautiful flowing stuff grannies used to wear, their merry faces poking out of mounds of billowy yardage? Those great ladies knew the value of keeping a few secrets. And if there were a few varicose veins and thick ankles mixed in among the better secrets, that's the luck of the game. Such problems don't disappear through over-exposure.

All this sounds, you say, like a fat old lady with bad legs talking. That may be, that may be. Last winter you could have found out just by looking. This winter will be more of a challenge.

Real Cool Cooler

We admit with disarming modesty that we can remember way back to the days when ice chests were being converted into refrigerators, and just as horseless carriages first looked like horseless carriages (as we can tell from pictures), so the first refrigerators looked like iceless ice chests—square insulated boxes in which to keep food cold.

That was then. The contemporary horseless carriage looks like a finback whale, if it's American—like a guppy, if it isn't. The contemporary refrigerator is something that I now feel compelled to describe in all its neurotic intricacy.

Ours is suspended from the east wall of the kitchen, and is a muted puce in color. It is short and wide with three magnetic doors without handles so it is anyone's guess whether they will open left or right. Inside is pink, and there are labels telling where everything goes. Behind sliding opaque plastic doors is a section labeled "vegetables," another for "fruit," and in one of the refrigerator doors are opaque plastic doors concealing the "butter" which is to lie on a plastic plate just the size for a quarter pound. If we conform and put the eggs in the door compartment saying "eggs" we may use plastic egg trays with indentations to conform to the contours of Grade A Medium eggs.

Now no one is going to tell us where to put our vegetables, fruit, eggs, etc. As for the butter—maybe we don't use butter. Maybe we use a euphemism to spread on our bread, and whose business is that of anyone's, let alone a puce refrigerator's?

To be friendly, however, we did put butter in the butter tray in the butter compartment the first day, and guess what happened. Apparently the temperature is supposed to be controlled in such a way that the spread is kept soft and spreadable. So the next morning all that was in the tray was a pool of melted butter. Well, Ghee Whiz, as Little Black Sambo would say. This feature clearly is the latest wrinkle, and it furrows our brow. It's like our dryer that has a sprinkler system. Things used to be hot or cold, wet or dry, light or dark, good or bad. No longer.

We saw right away the danger of being dominated by this strong mechanical assembly line personality. So we put meat in the vegetable place and eggs where the milk is supposed to go. The wretched refrigerator countered by running all night and freezing the milk which broke the bottles. The only way we could turn it off was to pull the plug.

Pulling the plug sounds simple. In the olden days one reached in back and gave a yank. Not now, by cracky. The nerve system and entrails of the contemporary hanging refrigerator are behind a puce facade above, high above, everything else, and consequently out of reach. Two agile fearless adults with timing, teamwork and a stepladder can unplug it in a few short minutes after they have figured out where it is.

Now it's our turn to counterattack, and we plan to chop the miserable appliance into a thousand little pieces, feed them into our nice new contemporary dispose-all, and eat out.

The Lights That Fail

Progress, in its relentless forward march, does not linger long among the by-ways where some of us make our burrows. It may be billeted with us for a short visit, but passes on. Our motels may boast that the March of Progress slept here, but for the most part our own slumbers are hardly disturbed by the rumble of its distant drum, though we sometimes may venture out to gather in the debris it has scattered along the way.

Among the latter are light fixtures. Lighting has come a long way since man first challenged the gloom with a simple torch, and it has, in my opinion, a long way to go. As with plumbing, heating and government officials, its promises are bright, its performances dim.

Intent on lighting the way to knowledge and truth, we bought a number of light fixtures last fall for our rejuvenated school. We spotted a few goose-necked desk lamps about in the library, and dangled hanging lamps shaped like flying saucers above the tables in the classrooms, the kind that move up and down, suspended from a cord. These last were, we felt sure, the ultimate in progressive illumination.

The school already had a number of electric bulbs functioning within a variety of ornamental disguises that recalled its shining past. Here and there were table, floor and pin-up lamps—ceiling bulbs hidden by chandelier dangles, a coachman's lamp in the Packet Room, opaque reflectors diffusing the glare in the dining room, ceiling globes in the kitchen. There were candles, too, on the hall table, and somewhere or other there is still a box of kerosene lanterns anticipating power failure. And of course the girls are required to have flashlights handy and on the ready.

On the ready. This could hardly describe our electric lighting arrangements, even when the Cape and Vineyard Company is its most companionable. The progressive debris that we have collected through the years fails to tackle the basic problem of getting the lights lit. We have bulbs—we have switches, but there seems to be no liaison between them. There are three switches in the back hall, yet the hall light switch is behind the dining room door. To turn off the front hall light you pick up a pot holder and unscrew the bulb. The light in the pantry flashes a series of Morse code distress signals whenever its switch is flicked. The obvious switch to turn on the light in the nurse's room activates the fire alarm.

The parking lot light switch used to be outdoors back behind the kitchen steps. If you donned foul weather gear, took your flashlight, groped through the blackened parking area and the shadowy sylvan glade and weren't decapitated by a clothesline, you might reach it within the half-hour, provided you knew where to look for it hidden beneath the ivy. Then you could enjoy having your way lighted back for you. We had it rewired to the housemother's study on the second floor, which makes it handy for the housemother, when she is in her study.

The flying saucer fixture in the English room turned on and off and slid up and down like anything until a few days ago when it gave up completely. Its lifeless corpse hung at the end of its tether a few inches above the table. John, the designated fixture fixer, studied the problem with a practiced eye.

"The trouble is," he said, "they've been yo-yo-ing it." He was right, of course. They had been yo-yo-ing, but Progress should take yo-yo-ing into account in designing lamps.

We can't blame East Brewster or the school for lighting difficulties. The same thing can go on in South Orleans, West Harwich or North Eastham. We *can* blame Progress for *sleeping* here, or point an accusing finger at whoever told Benjamin Franklin to go fly a kite. (Think of the trouble Charlie Brown gets into without benefit of a thunderstorm!)

The time has come to light the candles. The candle has inspired poets and needs no flying saucer to glorify it. The light switch in the French room sulks undiscovered behind a row of books. From the French room come youthful voices in melancholy strain: "Ma chandelle est morte; je n'ai plus de feu . . ."

So dies a good deed in a naughty world.

Decorum

Now is the time of year when we on the Cape must take our feet off the kitchen table, put on a clean pair of jeans and greet the summer folk with appropriate decorum. And now is when summer folk pile into the station wagon and come to the Cape to put on an old salty pair of jeans and put their feet on the kitchen table. Decorum is, after all, how you look at how you should behave when you want to look as if you knew how, right? Or vice versa.

This preamble is intended to lead decorously into a brief culling of excerpts from a volume of the late 1870s we found recently, entitled *Decorum: A practical treatise on etiquette and dress of the best American Society,* a poignantly philosophical banquet of advice of whose succulence we can give only a few morsels. It is the sort of book you like to read bits aloud from when sitting in the kitchen with your feet on the table. So before we remove ours—just listen to this:

p. 17 "When a man rises from his seat to give it to a woman, he silently says, in the spirit of true and noble manliness, 'I offer you this, madam, in memory of my mother who suffered that I might live, and of my present or future wife who is, or is to be, the mother of my children.' "

p. 44 "The etiquette of handshaking is simple. A man has no right to take a lady's hand until it is offered. He has even less right to pinch or retain it."

p. 98 "Avoid picking your teeth, if possible, at the table, for however agreeable such a practice might be to yourself, it may be offensive to others. The habit some have of holding one hand over the mouth does not avoid the vulgarity of teeth-picking at table."

p. 99 "Never pare an apple or pear for a lady unless she desire you, and then be careful to use your fork to hold it...It is considered vulgar to dip a piece of bread into the preserves or gravy upon your plate and then bite it."

This rule inspired me to create the couplet:
"More flagrant evidence of love we may not yet aspire to,
But you may pare a pear for me because I so desire you!"

p. 145 "Mr. Pullman, the inventor of the palace car, was asked why there were no locks or bolts upon the ladies' dressing-rooms. He replied that 'if these were furnished, but two or three ladies in the sleeping car would be able to avail themselves of the conveniences, for these would lock themselves in, and perform their toiletries at their leisure.' This sounds like satire upon our American ladies, but we fear it is true."

p. 66 Letter Writing. "Love's Declaration: Dear Miss Hill: I am conscious that it may be presumptuous for me to address you this note; yet feel that an honorable declaration of my feelings toward you is due to my own heart and to my future happiness. I first met you to admire; your beauty and intelligence served to increase that admiration to a feeling of personal interest; and now, I am free to confess, your virtues and graces have inspired in me a sentiment of love—not the sentiment which finds its gratifications in the civilities of friendly social intercourse, but which asks in return a heart and a hand for life....Believe me, dear lady, with feelings of true regard, Yours most sincerely, Harry Stover."

p. 167 "Answer: Dear Sir: Your note of the 10th reached me duly. Its tone of candor requires from me what it would be improper to refuse—an equally candid answer. I sincerely admire you. Your qualities of heart and mind have impressed me favorably and now that you tell me I have won your love, I am conscious that I too am regarding you more highly and tenderly than comports with a mere friend's relation. Do not, however, give this confession too much weight, for, after all, we may both be deceived in regard to the nature of our esteem; and I should, therefore, suggest, for the present, the propriety of your calling upon me at my father's house on occasional evenings, and will let time and circumstances determine if it is best for us to assume more serious relations to one another than have heretofore existed."

p. 179 "Love is a universal passion. We are all, at one time or another, conjugating the verb 'amo.' "

p. 189 "We believe all sensible fathers would sooner bestow their daughters upon industrious, energetic young men who are not afraid of days' work than upon idle loungers with a fortune at their command."

p. 283 "The bathing-dress should be made of flannel. A soft gray tint is the neatest, as it does not soon fade and grow ugly from contact with salt water. It may be trimmed with bright worsted braid. The best style is a loose sacque or the yoke waist, both of them to be belted in and falling about midway between the knee and ankle. Full trowsers gathered into a band at the ankle, an oil-skin cap to protect the hair, which becomes harsh in the salt water, and socks of the color of the dress complete the costume."

p. 319 "The Beard....Our advice to those who shave is like Punch's advice to those about to marry; 'Don't!' There is nothing that so adds to native manliness as the full beard if carefully and neatly kept. Nature certainly knows best; and no man need be ashamed of showing his manhood in the hair of his face. The person who invented razors libeled nature and added a fresh misery to the days of man. 'Ah,' said Diogenes, who would never consent to be shaved, 'would you insinuate that Nature had done better to make you a woman than a man?' "

p. 326 On Feet. " 'How dirty your hands are!' exclaimed an astonished acquaintance to Lady Montague, whom she met in public with hands most decidedly unwashed. 'Ah!, replied that lady, in a tone of the utmost unconcern; 'what would you say if you saw my feet?' "

And with that final observation we must, as we said before, take ours off the kitchen table...

Flea Marketing with Al

How it happened, Al had to go through all the stuff his parents left behind when they went to live overseas, and some of it wasn't worth shipping off, so what to do with it? That Al—I tell you—whatever he does he's got to get a couple of laughs or turn it into a happening, or get something out of it. I mean, going through old family stuff is really the pits. If you've ever done it you know. But Al, he throws together the good stuff and gets some guy in Chatham to crate it off for him, and takes the junk, sticks it in his van, and one Sunday morning before we're even up he's coming back from the Wellfleet Flea Market with the van empty and $40 in his jeans.

"My God, Al," we say.

"There's nothing to it," he says. "You just go early to the Wellfleet Drive-In and pay five bucks to go in and set up, and that's it. You should have been there. The stuff, you wouldn't believe, and the characters you see wandering around! You ought to go some time."

So next Sunday we go, with a few goodies of our own that had been gathering grime in the barn for 20 or 30 years, and Al goes with us with some bicycle parts he hadn't unloaded the first time and an oriental bird picture made of shells, some file boxes and a few travel books out of the '60's.

But that's not all. The day before, after going through the barn with Helen, collecting stuff, we find ourselves with a dump load, so we head for the dump, and there's this thing standing beside the big metal containers. It has its back to us, with an electric cord hanging out one side, and it is big—like about a yard by a yard. My God, what is it? So I sneak a look while Helen is crashing bottles in the glass bins. My God, it's an organ—an electric organ. It looks OK outside except for a hunk of veneer missing in front—all the keys are there, and it's heavy enough so we figure it hasn't been gutted.

"That's not guaranteed, you know," a guy shouts with a big laugh as we're driving off, but before we even get it into the house

Al has it plugged into one of the garage plugs, and after fiddling with a couple of wires he's got her playing "Oh, Suzanna," and "Flies in the Buttermilk," and a few disco numbers standing there on the blacktop with one foot on the pedal, so into the van she goes with the rest of the stuff.

How much do you charge for a dump organ? $15 dead, we figure—$50 if she sounds like she's being played by E. Power Biggs with Al at the controls—and that's the way she sounds. Well, nobody's going to pay $50 at a flea market for an electric organ that may not work, and there are no plugs handy at the Drive-In, but we know she plays so we put a $50 sticker on and there's no guilt trip, and we take along my tape recorder with a cassette of E. Power Biggs Favorites to play as a come-on. What the hell, if no one shells out $50 we get to keep the old dump organ and we still wind up ahead, especially if we can hang onto Al for a while.

So the morning dawns, foggy. What do you wear to a Wellfleet Flea Market? All those characters Al tells about—and we want to fit in. I say jeans and a workshirt as usual, the honest approach, especially since mine are half dirty already. Helen thinks an India print skirt, tank top and sandals will do more for sales, so we give it a little of both. Al has other things on his mind.

7 am. We wheel the '69 VW van toward Eastham and Wellfleet, loaded to the once-sliding roof, hoping the dump organ won't fall through the rusty floor. There's a suburban station wagon in front of us pretty full of junk in the rear, going into Eastham, so we follow it mindlessly, knowing it must be going our way. It turns off at the Sheraton.

It's 7:30, and there must be forty vans at the Drive-In before us, but still plenty of room for more. We get a pretty good spot, not far from the snack bar, and haul everything out. We have an old sheet to go on top of the card table and rusty metal serving cart, but forgot to bring the stickers to put price marks on. Al makes prices on a scratch pad he has, and tries to weight them down on the sale items, but they kind of flutter around a bit.

We take turns; two of us look around while one minds the shop and van. Right off, an oldish guy asks about the organ.

"Perfect tone," I say with conviction. "Wish you could hear it."

E. Power Biggs is just moving into "Sleepers Awake!" on the recorder.

"Have you got any violins?" he asks, looking around vaguely.

"Not today."

He tells us about his musical career, and winds up buying Al's oriental shell picture.

Then there's this lady who says she teaches school in Oster-ville, and buys one of Al's file boxes. Then she buys four glass salt cellars from my table, and tells me to hold the wine glasses for her. Ten minutes later, when it's my turn to walk around, I see them on her table ready to be sold for more. Greedy, I think, and it begins to get to me.

"We underpriced everything," I tell Helen, furious.

"Look," she says. "Nobody's buying them from her. Relax."

But it's a common ploy here, I realize, buying from one guy, blowing the dust off, and then selling again for twice as much.

We look at a huge school bus that takes two or three spaces, jammed with stuff that gets hauled out bit by bit and sold. That baby means business. "It was here last time I came too," Al says.

Most of the people we talk to say they come regularly, and regularly now means both Sundays and Wednesdays. There's a guy saying, "Here I am stuck with this," holding a big flowered Japanese lampshade while his wife arranges stuff on their table. There's a nice wooden panel with Dutch kids drawn on it. and a lady who says, "That's supposed to have been done by Basil Rathbone's wife. She designed a whole room like that, all Dutch." There's an old-bottle man with a nice display. Helen wants one of his $4 bottles (about the size of a thimble). He comes down to $3.50 just for her. She loves it. "But Helen," I say, "3.50!" "I know," she says. She buys it.

There's a thin line between the funky and junky. There's a hamburger press for people who don't like pressing hamburgers by hand. There are antique irons without handles, baseball cards, helmets, bright yellow macramé hangers for plants, plastic hangers for clothes. There are stuffed dolls, sandals, curtains, dishes, glassware, a rusty ice cream freezer, old birthday cards, Mason jars and lids, a printing set, tools, old typewriter ribbons, hurricane lamps, 25¢ books, 10¢ books, 3-for-$1 cookie tins and a picture of the Rest House In Swansea, Mass ($1).

One lady has some old fashioned whisks, the kind used for whipping eggs before the eggbeater. "They're cute hanging on walls," she says. "Better on your walls than mine," she adds dryly.

By 9 am we've sold a bunch of wine glasses and most of the dishes we bought, and some of Al's stuff. The fog, instead of lifting, is lowering, and the organ looks drippy. We pack up. All told we are $14 richer and a few pounds lighter, and if it hadn't been for the Wellfleet Flea Market we never would have picked up our dump organ. So it just goes to show!

Button Button

The other day we were privileged to drive Jimmy back to his Service Station in the boss's suave new Rambler.

"You really should get checked out in this," said Jimmy, "before you drive it," as he watched us flay the air with our right hand in search of a gear shift while the left faltered between wheel and a cluster of cold, impersonal pushbuttons marked D1, D2, etc.

We felt as if we were in a saucer in outer space without a driver's license.

And if you want to go into a tailspin, just push the D2 (high gear) and R (reverse) button at the same time. As if it made any difference, since the moment you step on the power brake (thinking it's a clutch) you go through the windshield anyhow!

It all caused us to cogitate on the love of humanity for pushing buttons. This is the pushbutton age and the more switchboardy we get the happier we are. "All you have to do is press a button" has become a catchphrase for our era which wants life to be one great automat. Our Utopia would be Robotia.

The Germans are with us in this, and with their mechanical genius are great ones for buttons to push. Way back in 1928 we remember going through the science museum in Munich with our sisters and brother pushing every button in the place, and it was loaded with them. We made things light up and whir around, and make noises. We made a model aerial railway go up and down its cable. Things buzzed, vibrated, and changed color at the touch of the smallest pinky on a button.

Delirious with joy, we went back to our hotel where our older sister and we were to share a room. On a small instrument panel beside our beds we found more buttons to press, and unable to read the German explanation of their function we began pressing them with abandon.

There was a considerable pause after we pressed one of them, so we tried again a couple of times to make sure it was in good working order. Nothing seemed to happen. Finally there was a knock at the door, and in came a chambermaid. We were flabbergasted! Our German was elemental in the extreme. Our sister, however, after mentally thumbing through the eight or ten words we had mastered came up with "Auf Wiedersehen." It accomplished our purpose and the genii disappeared.

There remained one button to be tried. We hovered over it for a long time, visualizing disintegration, or that it might make us shrink like Alice in Wonderland, or worst of all, bring the maedchen back again. Finally, on a dare, one of us pushed it. We heard a far-off click. It had bolted the door. Sick with relief, we went to bed.

—●

Consumer Reports

Gentlemen: Just reading *Consumer Reports* fills my window shopping needs, and makes me feel practical and economical, but this isn't my annual fan letter. Right now I want you to go bail for me.

I set out for the January sales with your new Buying Guide Issue under my arm, love in my heart, and a wallet in my jeans that was nicely filled out with Christmas bonuses. I never thought of Boston as a hostile town, yet here I am in the hoosegow, and no one seems to care or understand. I am writing you because I feel perhaps you will understand, and in the hope that you will care.

What happened is this: I headed for the department store area with two particular items in mind--molded luggage, and bed pillows. First the luggage. I found stacks of it taking up half a room in the first store I tried. Whipping out the Guide, I followed its instructions:

"...Check the frame's sturdiness by opening the case ninety degrees and seeing how hard it is to flex the edges; pull the lid sideways to see how readily it tends to deform...Try the handle for size and comfort. Pinch the lining in several places to see how firmly it is glued down..."

It was while I was still pinching the lining of a $45 twenty-six-inch case that the salesman accosted me. "Can I help you?" he asked between clenched teeth.

"Why no," I said, "as a matter of fact I find the linings of your cases are not well glued, and the lids don't stay open the way they should, so I shall have to look elsewhere."

He accompanied me to the elevator and pushed the button. My next quest before I left the store was for bed pillows. I had read all you had to say about shredded foam and waterfowl down, so when I approached the generously stacked counters I knew just what to do. I compared them for resiliency by placing them on a flat surface (the only one handy was the floor) and compressing them to about half their original thickness. I made sure the openings used for inserting the filler were well-closed with both ends of the seam backstitched (and not all of them were). I made it my job to "knead a synthetic fiber of feather-down pillow to determine whether its filling had uniform consistency," and at this point I was approached by the floor manager. He did not ask if he could help me.

"Watcha doing to our pillows?" he asked, his face flushed. In truth, the display case was in some disarray, and a few tiny goose down feathers were gliding softly between us.

"I was only giving them the necessary tests," I replied with hauteur. "They don't all measure up," I added. I balanced a couple of them on my arms, as you suggested, to see if the corners drooped, and then held them by the ends and shook them.

"See here" said the manager, "quit it!"

Indignantly I pointed to the section on page 96 of the Buying Guide that was giving me my instructions. "We must now fluff the pillow to see if they have good domed-shaped crowns," I pointed out, "and unzip the foam rubber ones to see if the filling is in one piece. We must make sure that zipper tapes are attached with two rows of stitching, tap and fold the ticking to see if it is heavily treated with sizing material, punch it and watch for signs of dust, and bury our face in it and sniff to see if the filler has been cleaned properly."

"Must we indeed," he said. "We'll see about that." I turned away from him and began to fluff and punch. "I'll bury your face in them for you," he shouted, and we soon had a brisk pillow fight on our hands (another effective test), until stronger authorities intervened. It seems the law was on his side, though Virtue and Righteousness were on mine.

This brings me to the spot where I now languish. I can only hope that the lawsuits which will ensue will turn out to be a Best Buy.

Please get me out of here.

Faithfully yours,

B.C.

Note: Consumer Reports reprinted this article in a following magazine issue, with illustrations, and added "The letter made us wince, but we enjoyed it nevertheless and think you will too."